# Shhhhh ... c
# tell my mot

*The Author (right) with her mum*

# Jennifer Wert

*Jennifer Bowler Publications,*
*October, 2019*

*Published by Jennifer Bowler Publications*
*First edition: October 2019*
*ISBN: 978-0-6486976-1-9*

This book is dedicated to my Mum.

She kept every letter I wrote home
and never once disowned me.

Thanks

To Sandy Coghlan, who pushed me into
this! Thank you for making me revisit
these long-lost times, mentoring me and
coaxing out all these words. You may live
to regret it. In fact I suspect you already
have - the formatting landed in your lap.
That'll teach you.

To Doreen and Alwyn. They both now
live in Melbourne, have grown up
families of their own and kindly gave
permission to pop their photos and my
version of our young lives into this book.

To David Bowler, the long-suffering
husband and artist in my life.

# Contents

## Chapter 1
# When It All Began
## 1962

*S.S.Stratheden, the ship we migrated to Australia on.*

My love of the ocean started in 1962 as a child of 7 migrating from England to Australia with my family, which consisted of Mum, Dad and my older brother, Robert. The farewell gift from school was the book, Robinson Crusoe, (strange present to give someone travelling by ship).

We were lucky enough to have a family 4 berth cabin on the P&O liner 'The Stratheden'. She was a beautiful ship and for me, a school free zone. There was a school on the ship, but mum said I didn't have to go if I didn't want to...so I didn't.

Instead my education consisted of exploring the decks, learning to swim in the pool and going up and down in the lift because I'd fallen in love with the lift boy.

Children had their own mealtimes and as I was a fussy eater, mum usually came into the dining room and between her and our very patient waiter, they found food that I would actually eat.

I don't recall going ashore too often but I do remember men with their little boats bobbing alongside our ship in Port Said and Aden selling all sorts of items. Ropes would be lowered to them and passengers would pull up the rope and then send money back to the sellers. (or probably the other way around, I wasn't into high finance back then)

My brother got a very noisy spaceship, very ethnic! I think this was a safe option because we were warned not to buy any local crafts such as padded foot stalls or toy camels made of leather as used bandages were often the stuffing. We do still have a couple of black ebony elephants and a brass Sphinx ashtray though.

Local police or custom agents would wander the decks and offer a prospective buyer a watch from the many that adorned their arms which were secreted under the sleeves of their jackets.

I also remember seeing real Arabs riding camels on the sand dunes that flanked the ship. This must have been going through the Suez Canal, we were told to make sure our cabins and port holes were locked because thieves could scamper up the side of the ship to board and rob us...thrilling!!

It was very hot, and my hair was always sticking to the back of my neck and I got prickly heat. The hairdresser on board gave me a cute little haircut. Off came the plats, no more ribbons or sleeping in hard plastic curlers which disguised my dead straight hair.

The new me, I loved it but that was short lived because when I paraded in front of the lift boy (the love of my life, he laughed at me) I went back to mum in floods of tears and she had to ask the him to tell me he really did like my new hairstyle and he was only joking.

Just to placate me, he gave me the very important job of looking out for his girlfriend. I was very happy to do this as it meant that he liked me again, only thing was, all the girls were his girlfriend, so I got a bit confused.

We did go ashore in Colombo. As my brother had been given a spaceship it was my turn now. The local children and women all wore brightly coloured and ornately decorated clothes.

Mum wanted me to have something as beautiful. I've never been one for pretty dresses and this shop was enough to turn me off for good.

We were lured into a dark and dingy store with the promise of many beautiful dresses. One was selected which had layer upon layer of tulle petticoats and on closer inspection, family upon family of fleas. We made a hasty retreat back to the ship.... Without the dress.

After Colombo it was just the ocean for days and days. I never saw the dotted line, but we did actually cross the equator. I know that's true because King Neptune came aboard, and I've still got the certificate to prove it.

Fremantle turned up one morning. We'd arrived in Western Australia. I just remember all these old ladies offering tea and cakes, nothing else. Wish I'd been more observant back then.

Melbourne on Friday the 13th of July was cold, rainy and a dark old winter's day. It didn't bother me too much as there was so much going on, but Mum was worried and disappointed. She'd been told by everyone, especially Dad, that this land was full of sunshine.

Clambering onto a bus with all our worldly goods and a whole lot of other people who wore the same expression on their faces as my

Mum, we were driven to a fenced in army camp with Nissan huts. HOME. How exciting. It was like actually living in a dolls house and what's more, we only had half of the hut because another family had the other bit.

Once our stuff had been plonked down, everyone was taken on a tour of the canteen where all the meals were cooked for us. It was bland food that even made my mum's; shall we say, *basic* cooking skills seem more homely and inviting.

The laundry rooms had big concrete basins, but I can't remember if there were any washing machines. The shower blocks were concrete buildings a bit of a distance from our hut, one for men and one for women. Sharing with total strangers? No problem there then.

I saw a man trying to chop down a tree because it had a wild creature in it. A possum, possibly poisonous and definitely a man eater. What was this country?

There were some swings and lots of other children who looked different to us and spoke funny. Found out they were Spanish and to me they were so beautiful.

The girls had their ears pierced and I so wanted to be as elegant as them. As my birthday was coming up and Mum had her ears pierced, she said that I could as well.

One Saturday morning Dad drove us into Coburg and Mum and I popped into the chemist where the man was going to do this amazingly wonderful transformation into beauty for me.

The tools of his trade were a very sharp needle and a cork. No ice, no anaesthetic, just needle, cork and brute force on my 8-year-old ear lobes.

I sat there very still as he did one ear. I think Mum nearly fainted.

Would I be brave enough to do the other ear?

Yes I was! Much to everyone's amazement. In went to gold sleepers and with a clean hanky to mop up the blood, a jar of Vaseline and instructions to keep the holes lubricated and clean I was sent on my way.

Driving back to the hostel my ears were getting hot and painful so not having the burden of seatbelts back then and our car had a sunroof, I simply stood on the back seat and the top of my body was wind surfing home. Ahh the coolness on my red-hot lobes was magic. The pain, puss and swelling did eventually go away.

School was a real downer, not the adventure I'd dreamed of. I knew that school in Australia wasn't going to be close to where we lived like our house had been in England.

Mum wouldn't be turning up at the school gate to take us home for lunch and be back in time for afternoon lessons.

I thought, well hoped really, that I could sit in a kangaroo's pouch and hold on to my sandwiches wrapped up in brown paper tied up with string.

My adventurous spirit soon wore off as I realized I had to climb on a bus with everybody else every day. Sometimes I couldn't get a seat and had to stand getting wobbled around or squashed.

The school was called Eastmeadows Primary School, but I couldn't see any meadows. The army camp we lived in was called Broadmeadows hostel and I think that was a lie as well.

There were lots of us children of different races in that school. I remember someone saying they were White Russians, Oh, what other colours do they come in I wondered.

My teacher was scarily horrible. It was the first male teacher I had ever seen, and he didn't like anyone that wasn't Australian. Funny that he was teaching in a primarily migrant school with just a smattering of Australian children from the housing commission area. He liked to demonstrate to us how he reached out the classroom window and smashed a snake to death with his 3-foot wooden ruler.

Would he also do that to a little English girl? What had the snake done to deserve that fate?

Another of my many reasons for fearing this man was that he liked to check what attire his inmates turned up to school wearing. I begged to always have my very best clothes on, which didn't amount to much.

Mum could never understand why I had suddenly changed into such a *Style Deva* on school days, yet I was a rough and ready tom boy the rest of the time. The reason was simple. If he liked what you wore, he was easier on you for the whole day.

One day, and only ONCE, I was selected and he first got me to stand by the side of my desk and said I looked very nice, then I had to stand on the desk seat so I was tall enough for my class mates closest to see how lovely I looked, then I had to stand on the desk itself, right up high and show the world my fashionable outfit in all its glory....only to be shamed in the most horrifying way when he spotted the shoes on my feet.

Spelling and I have never been of the same mind set. This was another of his greatest loves. 10 words were sent home with you every night and you had to learn them and spell them correctly the next day...or else! I can't spell and never have been able to do so. I tried learning those 10 words every day and I knew what was coming after dress inspection time.

**DREAD.**

He would call out each word and we had to write them down, my stomach would churn, and I'd be breaking out in a sweat. When it came time for him to check them, I'd always be excused to rush to sick bay because up would come my breakfast. There I'd stay until lunchtime and knew that it was safe to come out again because it was only arithmetic in the afternoon, and I was OK with that.

On hot weekend days or school holidays a lot of us hostel kids would go to the local outdoor swimming pool but one very hot day they shut it and wouldn't let anyone in.... because...... someone had LICE!!! I didn't even know what lice were, but a great fear spread throughout the entire hostel community and Mum tried to explain to me the horror of these giant crawling insects that devoured all of mankind. Or something like that anyway. That was enough to convince me that the local pool had to be off limits until the fumigation process had been completed.

Dad and Mum had put a deposit on a piece of land in Clifton Springs and it was going to be where they were going to build our new home. Dad had a car and he'd drive us there on the weekend and we'd see where our special piece of Australia was and then head down to a little beach that had a brick wall around it and we'd have a picnic. I liked going there even when we found out the sand on the 'Beach' had been trucked in and after a good strong tide the new sand simply washed away, and nice black greasy stuff was left behind. Oh well, the yellow stuff might come back one day.

On the ship coming over, Mum and Dad had made friends with an older couple who'd been to Australia before and actually had a house with a large bungalow out the back awaiting their return. They were gentle people and had gone back to England to tie up loose ends and now were coming back to live.

Gladys and Richard were their names but affectionately known as Glad and Dick. It became uncomfortable when someone said, "Hi Glad, how's your Dick?

They had a grown-up daughter who lived in England and probably wanted her to join them in Australia, but she was a young woman, happy with her life and chose to stay where she was. Our family was invited to live in their bungalow until we got properly settled.

How lovely was that?

Still Mum and Dad didn't want to be a burden and really not knowing what the future would bring declined their kind offer.

However, horror of all horrors! Hepatitis broke out at the hostel. It is a very contagious disease and can be fatal so when the offer again came from Gladys and Richard, Mum and Dad accepted it, and off to Frankston we went.

The bungalow was fabulous. One great big bedroom for all of us, then another room for preparing and eating meals and another room with a toilet and vanity basin. Would we need anything more? NO. Well only a shower which we had once a week in Gladys and Richard's bathroom.

Mum and Dad both got work locally in a factory making metal coils or some such thing. Robert and I could walk to school and the beautiful Frankston beach wasn't too far away.

I even had a kind and friendly teacher who took her time with me and helped with my woeful spelling. It didn't really improve but at least I wasn't sick to my stomach everyday anymore. Besides, she encouraged me to write stories and she knew that my Mum would correct my spelling before I'd hand it in to her.

Maybe she had a crystal ball and knew that spell check was coming in the future.

Life was perfect as far as I was concerned. Gladys and Richard didn't even mind when I begged for a dog that was in the pet shop window, they helped talk Mum and Dad into letting me have her. All this was fine for a child, but my parents really needed to get their own place.

Not too far away in the north of Frankston there is a housing commission estate, so our names were put down and we waited for a house. Meanwhile though, Dad had befriended a builder who needed a labourer.

Up for the challenge, a change of occupation for my Dad and that's what he became. One of the houses that Joe (the builder) and Dad built was our new home.

Being a child, I don't know the ins and outs of the transaction, but I remember that if Dad finished off the house and could get a bank loan it would be ours. And it was. No need for the commission house after all.

Our little cream brick veneer house was in the bowl of the cul-de-sac, the second house built in the street with wild native bush land right up to the back fence, accessible only by an unmade dead-end road.

We weren't completely out in the sticks, but we had a very long walk into the town along rough dirt tracks if the car ever broke down.

An occasional tiger snake or echidna would pay us a visit and every second year we'd get a swarm of black caterpillars smothering all the windows and fly wire doors. Kookaburras and magpies filled the air with their unique songs, and we kids became expert at street cricket, tree climbing and dragging as much dirt into the house as possible.

Dad was in his element. He now had his own large garden with vegetable patches, ornamental edges and a chicken run. Mum wasn't so sure. She was a Londoner through and through and missed the business of everyday life, the closeness of shops and her family.

She always hoped that in two years the family could return to England, but doubt was creeping in as Dad got more and more comfortable. Also, most of Dad's family got onto the migration band wagon and our little house was crowded out for quite a few years as they descended upon us.

*Let's skip a few years now.*

High School days are in the past and best forgotten. A career in hairdressing started out as an option but being an apprentice felt like it was little more than slavery.

Dermatitis savaged my hands from all the hair washing and the other hairdressers were always bitchy. It sort of lost its appeal after a while.

On Sundays I worked at a dog kennel which was my part time job when I was at school and never gave up even when I'd started my apprenticeship. However, both these jobs ended quite abruptly when I tried stopping a dog fight by prizing them apart with my hands.

Needless to say, the dogs included me in the affray resulting in a stay in hospital suffering blood poisoning, badly torn and swollen fingers and weeks before I could go back to work, so I didn't, well not hairdressing anyway.

Mum wanted me to go back to school but my pride got in the way. I did need to find a job though and that came about by an advert for a junior at the local supermarket.

It was actually fun. Everyone was so friendly, and the job was enjoyable, although the wages were low, not ridiculous like apprentice hairdressing low, but still just above child slave labour wages.

Working as a Check Out Chick was quite a taxing job back then. No such thing as scanning the bar code, you actually had to punch in the numbers and work out the change. Adding to this you had to learn the prices of the weekly specials off by heart.

Our staff room had them displayed on a shelf, so you even studied for your work in your own lunch hour.

There were store competitions for the fastest and most accurate operator. Plus, the customers always had their favourite and I'm so glad it wasn't ever me. The poor lady who earned that honour never seemed to get a break, she'd have a massive queue lined up just to go through her register and she never lost her temper or anything.

It really wasn't my style, so I started working in the delicatessen section. No more panicking about giving the right change or incorrect packing of the brown paper carrier bags like putting delicate items on the bottom and heavy things on the top such as potatoes shoved in after eggs.

Sometimes to earn more money I did the night stacking of the shelves. Muscle power was needed for that job and it was dusty and dirty work. I only ever asked to do this when completely broke or needed extra money for birthday or Christmas presents.

The rival supermarket had more alluring wages and as I now had experience to brag about it was inevitable that my loyalty would shift. Especially after they accepted my resume.

Finally, after just a few months of better wages and a promotion to manageress, money was resting in my bank account for the first time ever.

August came and it was a cold one, the winter had felt eternal. Time for a holiday.

Not having any idea where to go the local travel agent suggested a tour of Alice Springs and Ayers Rock. Fantastic!

Bravely taking off. Literally in an areoplane for the first time, then meeting up with total strangers all by myself was a bit daunting.

Within minutes of landing at Alice Springs airport, everyone was in awe of the heart of this great ancient land and we shared our wonder and excitement of the tour that was to come.

The Dreamtime stories, climbing Ayres Rock, horse riding, watching damper being prepared and cooked over the ashes of an open fire (let's not mention the ants that stumbled into the raw sticky mess before cooking) Kings Canyon, a locust plague with these huge insects flinging themselves at me and getting tangled in my long hair, flooding rain and helping the locals push a Mini Moke out of the boggy track that pretended to be a road. Loved it, loved it, loved it. Confidence was on an all-time high.

*Uh Oh, now what's happened?*

*Chapter 2*

# The Dream

## 1974

*A Koala in the Grampians. Halls Gap is a beautiful village
nestled in the Grampians National park*

There was a song constantly playing on the radio at this time which seemed to be giving me a warning. It was called; **Wild World** by Cat Stevens.

The love of the sea and the want, desire and in fact need to wander was eating into me. Youth fares of sea voyages to England were in reach.

On a Chandris line ship named S.S. Australis I booked my one-way passage to England. The sailing date was Sunday the 13th October. That meant shopping for warm clothes because I'd be arriving in England in winter and summer clothes including one or two new bikinis for the hot countries I'd be visiting on the way.

Oops, need a passport. A British passport complete with photo of myself quickly done in a lunchtime break (well it probably took a lot longer than that, but it felt like just a lunchtime).

I hadn't actually told anyone outside the immediate family of my travel plans but as time was nearing the departure date, I could hold my secret no longer.

Would you believe it? Two girls who worked in the same shop were also going to be taking off. We actually didn't know each other as we all worked in different departments but once the word got out the coincidences were even stronger. We were all booked on the same ship at the same time.

Doreen a small blonde-haired girl who worked at the front of Richie's supermarket. She was a Check Out Chick and occasionally stacked shelves. As I was again working in the deli, I hadn't actually met her in our day to day working lives.

Alwyn was the other girl and she worked in the office which was upstairs in the building across the road. She seemed a quiet person but friendly. As our travel plans had all been made separately, we wondered if we could get along together, safety in numbers, so to speak. Well we'd better get to know each other.

On the Queen's birthday long weekend, we decided to all go away together. Doreen had a car, so we all chipped in with petrol, Alwyn and another friend called Stacey and I took off to Halls Gap.

We booked a four bed room in a motel which was cheap enough split equally between us. The weekend consisted of clambering all over the Grampians, wandered to restaurants at night and listened to noisy grumpy koalas but more importantly we chatted and got to know each other.

Alwyn's brother, Grant, also took the long weekend as an excuse to have a motor bike ride to Halls Gap with his mates. This turned out to be fortunate for us four girls as Stacey unfortunately fell and injured her shoulder resulting in terrible pain.

The solution was for her to lie down taking up the whole back seat of Doreen's car all the way home. Grant offered to pillion one of us on his motor bike as there was only room for three in the car now.

Yep, that pillion passenger was me. I had a nice warm duffle coat, gloves and boots on but that did nothing to stop the freezing cold blasting into my bones. I now know why bikers wear leather gear.

The closer we got to Melbourne the more the traffic jammed but the bike was able to weave it way through. The girls, unfortunately, in the car with their ailing friend took about 3 hours longer to get home.

These days I think I would have suggested she was taken to the emergency department of the local hospital, even if it was only for painkillers.

# Chapter 3
# S.S. Australis
## Sail Away

*S.S. Australis. A Chandris line ship that started this adventure plus 45 more years of wonderful memories*

So excited. The day finally arrived, and I can't remember anything from the previous weeks. I know there were parties and farewells, but my focus was on the departure date and everything else is erased.

Dad drove the car, Mum, Robert and I were the passengers. As we neared Station Pier driving along Beaconsfield Parade the sight of the ship made my heart beat faster, but I hid the fear that was clenching my throat.

Was this ship large enough to tackle the wild seas all the way to England? I'm sure the ship we came out to Australia on back twelve years earlier was a lot larger, or was it that I was simply a lot smaller?

Obviously when I'm excited or scared my brain falls out because I don't remember all the paraphernalia that goes on before boarding, I just remember searching and finding our cabin and then Doreen, Alwyn and some other girl named Denise with their friends and family all clambering for a space in our cabin.

When the call went out for all visitors to leave, I had a chill run down my spine, Mum was crying and Dad has a clenched jaw, we all knew how each other was feeling, excitement was giving way to fear but too late now.

It was dark by the time the ship finally sailed and we waved to each other until they were out of sight. That's when the chilliness of the night-time air made me stop watching the car lights flickering along the coast back to Frankston.

Mum mentioned in her first letter that they watched the ship all the way down to the heads. (which is the entrance to Port Phillip Bay) I know Mum desperately wanted to be going 'home' with me. Dad would have loved to be back at sea working once again as a merchant seaman. Time had moved on and life commitments had changed. It was now my turn for the adventure.

In our cabin everyone chose which bunk they wanted. Doreen and Alwyn both had the lower ones and Denise and I had the top ones. Luckily, we three friends could share a cabin and Denise, even though a stranger, seemed easy enough to get along with as well.

Once that was sorted, we went exploring the ship then came back and decorated the cabin with the streamers, balloons and cards we'd all received, a real party cabin now, just hoped we wouldn't get told off.

Then in came our cabin steward, he seemed nice, but his teeth were black with a couple of gold ones and he has a very hard name to pronounce, it was something like Yukavous so we asked if we could just call him Yukky. He laughed and said yes. I think he thought he was in luck with 4 girls all in their early 20's to take care of, it would have been a case of "Call me anything you like!"

Sleep came pretty quickly and easily on that first night. The cabin was warm, and we were all exhausted.

The next morning, we found the dining room and had breakfast about 9.30am. Doreen, Alwyn and I were all allotted different dining tables so we asked if we could sit together and they shuffled a few people around so we could. Now we were sharing with a lady called Elaine a man called Bill and his daughter Jackie.

The rest of the day consisted of wandering around and getting hopelessly lost then elated when we found out short cuts to the bars and our cabin. A passenger who had obviously done this trip before had a slide show which was interesting and gave me ideas of what to do and where to go when we arrived at different ports. There were plenty of things to do whilst at sea, sometimes for days on end, so I planned on doing as much as possible.

We were warned the first day at sea was lifeboat drill and it was mandatory to attend. The alarm bells and horns as well as someone yelling over the PA in both Greek and then English was enough to make you want to jump overboard. We all had to put on these bright orange life jackets and waddle up on deck, I now know what it feels like to be either fat or pregnant. We all thought it was a bit of a laugh, but the crew seemed to take it all very seriously though, thank goodness.

Sydney was our first port of call, but we had a day at sea before we got there. Even though it was sunny the wind was cold up on deck. Warmer countries to visit on the way were a promise. That was something we all looked forward to.

Beautiful Sydney harbour welcomed the S.S. Australis and her disembarking migrants as well as the rest of her passengers. It was a glorious sunny morning when we docked. Doreen, Alwyn and I decided to do a self-tour of this beautiful city.

We wandered over to the Australia Square building, which is actually round and went up the 48 stories in an elevator that almost made our ears burst with its speed and we clung to the walls, great views from up there though, so totally worth it.

Later mooched around the huge library, took in the beauty of the parks and then over to the brand new, one-year old famed Sydney Opera House. The roof lines really looked like sails and the gleaming whiteness almost took our breath away. I met the head waiter of one of the many restaurants who signed a menu as a souvenir for me and then said to come back for a free drink next time I'm in town. That'll be a while!

A hydrofoil was waiting at Circular Quay, so on we hopped and off to Manly we went. Such a beautiful harbour no matter which way you looked, and it was a glorious day but chilly on deck.

Being total tourists, we took in all the sights plus browsing through Corso markets I bought a soppy blue and white checked hat. There were many marked walking tracks, but we needed to get back to the main city, so we grabbed another ride in the hydrofoil then back to the ship for warmer clothes before exploring the seedier side of town, Kings Cross. I'd never seen sex shops before but felt quite safe on the bus ride that we'd taken. I remember laughing at an old bloke who could hardly walk make his way into one.

The sun was setting, and the ship was due to depart so time to get back on board. More new passengers boarded and looked as lost as we had only two long days ago. The streamers, tears and waving goodbyes were done all over again but this time I didn't have the same feeling of being scared and alone.

The gong chimed calling us for dinner. Our table waiter was an Indian guy who invited Doreen, Alwyn and I back to the cabin he shared with some other waiters. We were a bit scared but also inquisitive, so we said OK.

It was really smelly down in the crew quarters; we think they cooked up their own curries. In no time at all we seemed to be surrounded by a group of young guys in very casual clothes and slip on shoes, nothing like what they wear in the dining room that's for sure.

We were offered Hand Jobs". **WHAT!!** Everyone insisted that they were palm readers ...*PHEW!* So we said they could read ours.

My reading was, *I'd be divorced, then marry again and that time I'd be cherished and have 3 children. I will live until I'm 80 and in 3 years' time come into money.* Well I have 2 children and hopefully last more than 80 years providing I stay healthy. I'm still waiting for the money to come my way. Maybe he didn't mean money. He may have meant riches because if that's the case, that part of his prediction was true.

We didn't stay down there long as it was stiflingly hot, not very comfortable and beginning to get rather crowded. However, we were constantly asked back, but we always declined. Aditya, one of the younger waiters kept chasing me up the stairs but it was all in fun (I think) and as they aren't allowed any higher than the Main Deck all I had to do was run up one extra flight of steps and he would never catch me.

Although I was sure it was safe, I later learned that it wasn't just fun they were after. Forty-five years later a man was seeking the whereabouts of his father as he was the result of a shipboard not so innocent infatuation.

Elaine, Jackie, Bill and I took it in turns to play deck tennis. It was great fun, but the sun can be a bit brutal out on deck, so a sunburnt face and shoulders was my payment. Didn't actually have sun block cream back then, either lather yourself with oil to basically cook or hide in the shadows only popping into the sunshine for brief fleeting moments.

Somehow, I managed to build up a suntan without getting too burnt in the process.

Washing our clothes was a slightly tricky business. We could wash our smalls in our room and hang them in the shower, but the other clothes had to go to the laundry. It felt like the bowels of the earth and always steamy and hot down there. I made friends with the Greek girl who worked in the laundry.

She would look after my clothes for me if they took too long to dry. Her name was Sueya and always wore a smile, even though we couldn't speak each other's language we managed to make ourselves understood with sign language of sorts. I hope she was able to learn English because she could become a stewardess and work in a nicer environment.

We had a new waiter on our table. His name was Nick and a Greek this time. I told him I didn't like the coffee much, so he made me a cup of Nescafe specially.

Before leaving Australia, Aunty Maureen told me the food would be all greasy and Greek, but she was wrong, the food was delicious, and our menu changes every night with lots of options to choose from.

The men who work on the ship seemed very nice but over sexed, they don't go around pinching you on the bum though as Aunty Maureen said they would.

The guys must think that all the single 20-year-old girls are fair game. I suppose we were really. The male crew constantly invite you down to their cabin and if you say no straight away they don't accept it but if you say 'maybe' and then duck out the way every time you see them, they finally give up. I got this down to a fine art eventually.

One step past Innocence' but way behind Women of the World. A steep learning curve was on its way.

The nights are full of entertainment in the Ballroom with dancing after a show or in the disco. There was a Maori concert with great costumes the night before we arrived in Auckland New Zealand. The men seemed quite intimidating the way they huff and puff and poke out their tongues. The women dancers were quite gentle compared to them.

I had a secret admirer. He bought me a drink. I checked him out but disappointingly he was only a little guy, not quite my type but nice enough. We girls had been gathering friends, so Stewart joined our merry band.

Arriving in Auckland we had another sunny day and six of us went on a tour. It was very interesting, but the tour was a bit bland, I think after seeing Sydney and all its beauty Auckland didn't hold much interest for me. Still that's not to say we didn't enjoy ourselves because we all enjoy each other's company anyway.

The ship was taking on more passengers and a whole lot of English and European people were leaving to start a new life.

We got the good deal, the young ones ready to travel and see the world. Fare welling New Zealand was just as much fun as Melbourne and Sydney with all the streamers and waving crowds. That time it didn't feel sad at all, I was enjoying shipboard life with all its carefree fun days and nights.

The Captain's Cocktail party was next on the entertainment schedule. This was the reason the travel agent advised us to take along at least one evening gown.

It was great fun dressing elegantly, giving each other the thumbs up on how beautiful we could look if we really tried. Alwyn was seeing quite a lot of George, the chief steward.

When it came to the obligatory professional photo, we decided that a group one would suit us all. Our photo has Elaine, Alwyn, George, Me and Doreen in that order.

The hors d'oeuvre were small little tasty nibbles but very hard to get more than one, it seemed like the people closest to the entry door for the waiters, just swooped and devoured as many as they could shove in their mouths at once.

Same happened with the free drinks. Quite mad really when you think dinner wasn't far away and free anyway.

The dinner menu was also special, and the waiters kept telling us how beautiful we all were. That night we all danced with a little more grace and elegance than we previously had.

October 21st, we reached Suva and it was hot. There was a Police band welcoming us and they all wore skirts with jagged hems.

Instead of taking an organized tour, the six of us dining room friends hired a car and Bill did the driving. Buying a map and just hoping for the best we came across a small village where people actually lived in beautiful little grass houses.

The native people are very dark brown with black afro hair. Lots of the people actually wear skirts, both the men and women. The children all seem so happy and carefree. They all go to school but no need for shoes.

Heading into the town we noticed that the shop owners were mainly Indian. They were very persistent in wanting us to buy from them. I was told you had to barter and get the prices down. That was very scary as I'd never done that before. I did end up buying a cassette radio recorder and bartered him down by $20 but probably still paid way too much.

At the docks lots of stalls were set up and Alwyn bought a beautiful Fijian costume which looked fabulous on her. I wish I'd bought one but then again, what would I do with it in England.

As the ship left Suva the Fijian Police band played a farewell tune. It wasn't until later that evening we realized Doreen had got sun stroke and wasn't well at all. I was sunburnt and suffered from it the next day. Luckily Doreen got over her sun stroke with a day of rest and plenty of cool drinks. That hot sun was something we were just not used to.

Out at sea for a few days, heading towards Mexico. My deck tennis was starting to improve, and I also took up dancing for the cabaret shows. There were two dances that needed to be learnt. All a bit old fashioned but fun for a cabaret I suppose.

They were *Down by the Riverside* and *When the Saints Come Marching In*. Michael the dance instructor/entertainment guy seemed really pleased with me and asked me to do a few more dance routines along with seven other girls. There were also guys in the dance group so that made it more fun.

With all of us together including Michael we numbered twenty. Cliff, one of the dancers was also a deck tennis player so sometimes after rehearsal we'd run around the deck a few times just for the exercise and then have a game.

**Latitude 00000, Longitude 142.50** (or thereabouts)

Yes, it was the 25th October and King Neptune has boarded the ship. At 1.15 pm just before lunchtime the announcements over the PA system tell us where we are and at what depth the sea is. This day we are 2,500 fathoms deep and crossing the equator.

King Neptune and all his disciples gathered around the swimming pool; a table was set up ready for the initiation ceremony. White gunk and red slime were splattered all over the unsuspecting souls before being slung into the pool. We all cheered, and I thanked god it wasn't me. The King has also chosen a Queen.

Having survived the ordeal, we were given a certificate signed by no lesser being than Davy Jones and Neptunus Rex themselves. What an honour.

That night in the Ballroom I was one of the Royal slaves. Dressed in a black piece of cloth tied around the side of my hips and a red top tied in the middle. I must admit that I didn't fill the top out as much as the other slaves, but I was passable. The show was a success and luckily, I gave Stewart, a Scottish friend, my camera and asked him to take photos of us all. This was really a fun filled day and everybody got involved one way or another.

The next day after dragging myself out of bed mid-afternoon, it was time for more rehearsals. This time we're in for the big show. I'm in no less than five numbers and we have to do everything twice for the two dinner settings. I remember being so nervous.

The costumes were very skimpy, a bikini with a tiny sarong wrapped around the hips. The theme was Hawaiian, and the songs are from the musical *South Pacific*.

We had a couple more days to get this right, but I had my doubts, we were all amateurs and it showed.

Wednesday 30th October. I didn't eat anything all day. Stage fright was at its height and I wasn't the only sufferer. Even Michael who directed the shows thought he might have been a wee bit ambitious this time. Well we didn't let him down.... the first show was a complete disaster, even the singers and the band mucked up.

This was when we saw what the wrath of a gay musical director could be like. YIKES!! What's worse though, we still had one more show to do.

At 10.30pm the second show went on, the blokes whistled and cheered as we skimpily clad girls gyrated with our hula attempts, the songs were sung properly, and the band kept up. This time it was a success and the euphoria was contagious.

Stewart had my camera again and he clicked away. Mind you, when the photos were developed you could see where he aimed the camera...and it wasn't at my face. Oh well, at least I've got proof that my 20-year-old body had all its bits in the right place.

I decided after that mammoth effort I'd give the dancing routines a miss for a while and get more deck tennis in. Besides we soon would be seeing land again and the excitement is building.

We would be docking in Acapulco, Mexico.

Nick, our table waiter and I have become a little more than friends. The Greek waiter's cabins were a lot nicer than the Indian waiters' ones and they didn't stink of curry. The guys had erected curtains around their bunks so there was a hint of privacy and hoped no one was listening when they had visitors.

In Acapulco, Nick said he would hire a car and a group of us would go sightseeing together. At 9.30am we met up and along with two more waiters and we went ashore.

This time we didn't actually dock, instead the ship was anchored out and we had to go ashore on motorized lifeboats, this is called a tender. At least I knew now that the little boats don't sink and weren't just painted onto the chains that held them in place on the side of the ship.

It took between 5 and 10 minutes to get us ashore once they'd loaded enough passengers into them.

From there we took a taxi to the hire car place and Nick hired a Volkswagen Safari. It was beaten up old thing which had seen better days. As it rattled and chugged along, we had to hold the down the roof for fear it would blow off. It felt so weird driving on the wrong side of the road and the steering wheel on the left.

Nick drove us into town and showed me the expert way to barter with the Mexicans. I wished I'd known how to do that properly in Fiji.

Unfortunately, the waiters had to get back to the ship in time for lunch service but would be back as soon as possible afterwards.

I couldn't understand why the passengers stay on board when we'd been at sea for days, surely, they'd want to wander around and see these exciting places.

I remained on shore souvenir shopping. Every time I bartered down whatever I purchased to a good price, the Mexicans wanted a kiss, it was a real laugh. It was one sure way to stop overspending.

After about an hour and a half I met up with a couple of passengers, one was Stewart, the Scott who had taken the photos for me with my camera. We went to a café and had some cake, and then he bought me a hat with Acapulco embroidered on it.

The lunch service was over, Nick, his friend, another Nick and girlfriend Patty and I met up and we climbed back into the hire car for a scary mountain cliff drive. The old car actually made it. From a vantage point you can see a procession of young men marching along the road leading up to the sheer cliff face.

Two or three of them climb to a ledge and then at the same time dive off into the tiny inlet of seawater between the ragged rocks below. It's a heart stopping moment, especially as we were told many of the divers have died doing this. It was thrilling. Mental but thrilling.

At the top of the mountain Nick asked if I wanted to have a drive of the old rattily car, so naturally I said yes. I thought he was joking but he climbed out of the car and we swapped seats. It wasn't until we were safely back down the mountain that I told him I didn't have a driver's license and I'd only ever practiced with my Dad next to me.

It's fun watching everyone's faces go ashen. Once they'd recovered, we headed for a glass bottom boat tour. It was fascinating seeing wild tropical fish which were the same species that Dad had in his aquarium at home but many times larger. One of the tour guides dived overboard and fed these fish so we could all get to see them clearly.

The boat glided over the water and then a huge golden woman's face peered up at us. It was so creepy. The face belonged to a statue of the Madonna that had fallen from a ship. It is said to be cursed because whoever tried to retrieve it has died. I suppose we've all got to go sometime. There were great big creepy looking crabs scuttling over the rocks on the banks as well. They looked like Giant spiders.

Once again, the guys had to get back to the ship, so Patty and I stayed ashore shopping until our money had run out and it was time to take the tender back to the ship.

Another day at sea and another day of fabulous fun.

Friday the 1st of November was Fancy Dress Night. Doreen and her new boyfriend Keith went as Hiawatha and Pocahontas, they looked brilliant especially as they both had good suntans now. Alwyn wore her Fijian costume and didn't have to do much to it to make herself look beautiful and for 3 days Cliff, two twin boys about 12 years old named Johnny and Danny and I teamed up and made a very impressive horse complete with chariot accompanied by Julius Caesar and Cleopatra.

We made the whole chariot out of cardboard decorated with ring pulls from beer cans, crepe paper, wool and it even had cardboard wheels which rotated on a broom handle. We nicked the broom from the cabin steward without telling him. The boys were our horse with a cardboard head and a sheet body, Cliff was Julius and he wore a white dress made out of an improvised bed sheet with skirt adornments made out of neck ties and I had a long black wig made of crepe paper complete with a headband sporting an asp. My dress was a long piece of fabric wrapped around and safety pinned in place.

It's amazing what you can do with reels of sticky tape and coat hangers. As we entered the room everyone cheered, the boys were crazy funny and hammed it up beautifully. Of course, we won, and I think about a million photos of us were taken.

The best photo was the professional one though taken by the ship's photographer. He was even impressed, and he's seen many fancy dress parades before. Cliff was the brainchild of this creation. I'm glad he chose me to be Cleopatra. The captain presented us with presents which the boys kept. I can't even remember what they were.

The fancy dress parade got people's imagination fired up and some of them were hilarious. One woman came with knickers pinned to her bra.... She was a *Chest of Drawers*. A mad funny guy came wrapped completely in plastic and shaving cream all over the top of his head.... He was a *Used Condom*! Someone else had tied balloons all over herself, she was a *Bunch of Grapes* and as the balloons began to pop, she became simply, *Haemorrhoids*.

All classy stuff.

As I said before, I decided to give up dancing and now it was my turn to enjoy the show from a comfortable seat.

We had a Greek night which started in the dining room and all the waiters were dressed up and a special menu went with it. The show with classic costumed Greek women dancers then the fellows had a go all in costume and the band was terrific.

By this time, I think we were friends with everyone on the ship. The constant sexual prowling of the male species waned as we became couples and we just enjoyed the company of who we chose, so much easier.

Another night the theme was Mexican, and Cliff was still in the dance troop. He was doing really well and thoroughly enjoyed himself. After the shows we always had dancing, most of the time I stay around.

One particular night I wish I hadn't though. The dance floor was packed, and we were up having a great time when this stupid drunken Aussie started flicking his head around and the back of his head collided with my face.

I was knocked out and splattered to the floor. My lips and nose were a bloody mess and I had to be carried back to the cabin. It took two full days for the swelling to go down, thank goodness for makeup to hide the black under my eyes.

Glad it didn't happen before any of the shows I been in. The guy who did this came and apologized the next day when he'd sobered up.

He was shocked by my swollen face and felt very guilty for marring my beauty. I looked like Barbara Streisand if she was a battered wife.

Yet another highlight of this voyage is the magnificent Panama Canal. We arrived here on the 4th November and I didn't want to miss the entry so going to bed was out of the question.

Only problem, I was talking too much with my friends at the bar and missed it. We were all disappointed with ourselves but not to worry because it takes ages to get through and the scenery is magnificent.

There are lots of little islands and the green vegetation is deep and lush. Alligators or crocodiles, I'm not sure which or maybe even both live down in these waters so going for a dip isn't such a good idea.

Some of the engineers offered to throw me overboard as I like animals so much, how kind. It's really interesting watching the ship get lifted up with the water, going through a lock then waiting for the next lift. It's a slow process.

The Pacific is higher than the Atlantic Ocean, but we still had to be lifted about 26 meters to get over the Panama terrain.

In the afternoon we were able to go ashore in Cristobel. From the ship everything looks beautiful but once ashore it's a different story. It's dirty with loads of beggars, prostitutes and thieves.

We were warned to go ashore in a group and watch out for each other. They slit handbag straps and men's pockets to steal your money. One of the ship's crew, a barman was held at knife point whilst they stole $150 and a policeman was standing very close and simply looked the other way.

We decided to go to a Hotel called the Washington as it was safer in there. It wasn't far away but the cab driver charged a lot of money. One of the guys called a policeman over and he sided with the taxi driver. Nothing we could do about it. Then the rest of our group turned up in another taxi and they were charged even more.

The hotel wasn't all that exciting and we were feeling brave enough to take on the wild streets of Cristobel providing we stuck together. As we knew where we were it was easy enough to walk back to the ship.

On the way we passed boys making one hell of a racket with homemade drums from tin cans, young girls with brightly coloured hair rollers as decoration in their tight afro hair. Alwyn picked up one little girl and gave her a cuddle, she had such a sweet face, I wonder what life has been like for her now that she'd be a grown-up woman. The children all seemed happy, at least to us anyway.

The waiters in our group had to go back to work, the twin boys, Johnny and Danny who'd been with us all day had to keep their promise of being back in time for dinner. So, the rest of us just hung around taking in the sights, found a restaurant for a taste of the local cuisine and kept in mind we had to be back on board by 10.30pm.

Whoops! Time had got away from us and it meant a mad dash.

Made it!

However, we then found out the pilot who steers the ship through the canal had rammed her into the dock and left a dirty great hole in the side. The makeshift repairs were underway which meant we could all go ashore again as long as we were back by midnight.

To this day I don't know why I wasn't worried. We still had a large ocean to cross and a whacking great hole in the side of a ship isn't the best remedy for a safe journey. I just figured that they'd fix it. Must have done because we didn't sink and I'm still here.

Back again on shore we headed for the casino. I'd never been inside one before and found the amount of money being splashed about astounding. One guy was betting $20 a time and loosing fiercely. No wonder the casino guys drive big cars and are snappy dressers.

We returned to the ship in time but again there was no hurry as we didn't sail until 9am the next morning.

Jim, one of the officers said that he'd been around the world 28 times and Cristobel was the worst place. He said they would slit your throat for 2 cents. I can quite believe it but luckily our group didn't have any mishaps...or 2 cent pieces.

Leaving the Panama Canal, we ventured into the Caribbean Sea and the sun was lovely and warm the colour of the sea was a beautiful deep turquoise. We didn't dock on any of the islands which was a shame.

Once through the Caribbean the ship headed towards Miami. Fort Lauderdale actually. This is the second last port before England. The weather was still warm and the ocean darker. Doreen and Keith seem to be getting quite serious with their relationship. He was a nice guy. Alwyn was off with George the chief steward who's quite a lot older than her but that's OK.

Cliff bought me a Brandy Alexander which looks like a chocolate milkshake but boy was it potent! I wonder if he had evil intentions...Hmm, looking at photos of him now, it's a shame he didn't, he was always a real gentleman.

Denise had disappeared from our cabin completely. Hadn't seen her for ages. No one has reported anyone overboard so maybe she has a boyfriend tucked away somewhere.

Yukkie, our cabin steward has turned out alright after all. He always knocked before coming in and tiding up our mess. He still had a problem with sweating when he had to duck under the line of drying knickers that hung in the shower on our makeshift clothesline. And the smile never leaves his face if one or all of us were still in bed when he called around. He was pretty old though, probably in his late 30's I should think.

It was evening when we arrived at Fort Lauderdale. I was supposed to go ashore with Nick, but his friend kept him waiting and I was too impatient to hang around so went ashore with Doreen, Keith and some other people.

The roads here are very wide and I noticed that the cars are as well. We went to one of those kiosk diners which you see on American TV all the time. I can't remember what I ate, probably just an ice-cream.

A couple of American guys in a sort of truck/ute combo asked if anyone would like a free tour. I was game and so was Alwyn, so in we hopped, and they drove us to Miami beach. We were a bit disappointed as our beaches at home were more impressive than this little strip of sand.

We kicked about a bit there before they drove us to their apartment which was the penthouse, so the views were beautiful with all the twinkling lights of the city. The guys were nice and it's funny the strange things you remember.

They had trays full of book matches. One of the guys collected them, so guess what they got from Mr Chandris, via us as a thank you for the tour? They then gave us both a box of 6 perfumes as a souvenir and we noticed it had a price of $50 on it. That was a fortune back then.

Apart from meeting these two really nice guys, Miami and Fort Lauderdale was a disappointment. It probably didn't help being there only in the evening and night and sailing away at dawn. Also, I'd forgotten to post a huge letter that I'd been writing to mum and dad and it will be days at sea with no chance of them getting any mail before reaching England.

The mood was changing with us happy go lucky 20+ year olds. The carefree days at sea were coming to an end. The future was a mystery that we had to confront.

Michael the entertainment guy had one last ditch effort at keeping his increasing glum passengers happy.

Vice-Versa night.

That brightened us all up. There's something about guys dressing up as women. They always go for the Tarty look. Stewart and I teamed up and he sat on my lap for most of the night. We were a good-looking couple but the best one was Alwyn. She had a black wig and drew a beard and moustache onto her face with eyebrow pencil, I think she borrowed the white shirt and black suit from George. All she did was simply sit there and look menacing. Creepy.

Not much happening out on deck anymore. It's too hard to play deck tennis with the wind whipping around. I love the rough seas, but it was cold outside.

Everyone started to swap the skimpy sunshine clothes for warmer cover ups. Most people had their excess luggage down in the hold and they had to scout around for their belonging, unpack and repack to get the warmer clothes out. I don't remember doing that at all that, but I must have because in a letter home I mentioned that I had to go back to Southampton to collect my suitcase that had been in the hold.

Rotterdam was the last stop before the final disembarkation in England. It was cold, rainy and trying to walk on dry land after all those days at sea was a riot.

Christmas lights were being put up and everything glistened. It wasn't late in the day, but it was very dark.

Denise our missing cabin mate returned, so she hadn't fallen overboard or met with foul play after all. The four of us headed to the most beautiful cake shops we'd ever seen. Had hot chocolates in a café and then bought eight cakes back to the cabin and had a gluttonous feast. Each cake cut into quarters so we could sample everything. Cream oozed out and the most delicious messy delights had never been experienced by any of us before.

Now we knew that if we didn't like England, cakes were waiting for us just across the channel.

Our last day of carefree reckless freedom has arrived, it was November 17th. The ship berthed at Southampton docks at midday, but nobody disembarked until 5pm when it was cold and dark.

I was being met by my two uncles who are my dad's brothers. I had seen them as a child and vice versa, now we had to search the waiting crowd looking for some sort of old recognition.

Doreen and Keith are heading off together and Alwyn has pre-arranged plans, whatever they were.

I was the only one of us girls with an address so I gave it to Doreen and Alwyn, also Stewart was going back to his adoptive parents in Scotland and insisted that we try as hard as we possibly could to come up and stay for Hogmanay. That seemed like a good plan. Why not?

Lots of tearful goodbyes to our shipboard families and lovers. Out into the cold evening ready to take what the world has to throw at us.

**Here We Come!**

*Chapter 4*
# Dad's Family
## Side-Stepping

*Most of my Dad's family when they were young. The eldest sister is missing from this photo. It is the only photo I have of them all together.*

Before we get started with the rest of my story, I'll take a little sideways step into the make-up of my Dad's family.

Dad was the fourth child in a litter; I mean family of ten siblings. One sister died at a young age from diphtheria, but she was always counted. Seven boys and remaining two girls.

Five of the brothers and two sisters migrated at different times to Australia complete with families of their own. Even my grandparents were able to migrate although they were way too old to work anymore. Remaining in England were the two Batchelor brothers. Uncle Ray and Uncle Alan.

Uncle Ray was known as the professor, simply because he liked reading. The family claimed he had a great wit and a quick comeback line.

Uncle Alan was the youngest and never mentioned much at all, I think they forgot he was around, who wouldn't when there were 10 of them.

Anyway, when I announced my plans of leaving the embrace of the family home, my father said I should go to Uncle Ray (from here in he will simply be known as Ray...enough of the old-fashioned niceties).

Apart from being a real wag and fun-loving guy, he still actually lived in the same house that the entire brood was brought up in. Therefore, my dad still considered it his home so I should be able to bunk down there without any further ado.

When I arrived at Southampton, however, and spent quite some time tracking my relative down in that shed full of total strangers I actually didn't know what he looked like. Should have asked for a recent photo of him before I left home I suppose.

Anyway, in the end I found a man who looked a mixture between my Uncle Charlie and Uncle Terry so I figured it could be the man I was after.

With great confidence in my deducing capabilities I approached this man and asked if he was looking for me, which he answered in the affirmative. Only problem was, it wasn't Ray, it was the well forgotten Alan. We said our Hellos and then took me to the correct uncle who looked nothing like anyone else and completely different to what I expected.

Mind you he said the same about me then showed me the photo mum had sent. In that photo I was buggering about pretending to eat dog food out of a can with a spoon. Why that photo? Mum said it was because she couldn't get a good one of me, but anything would have been better than that!!

My suitcase still hadn't emerged from the hold so with just the small bag of clothes and some souvenirs we headed for home. I'd be back for the case later.

Ray asked, "Why are you going to stay with me?" and it wasn't said with a smile.

My answer of course was that Dad told me to.

Now back to my story.

*Chapter 5*

# England Part One

## Far Away From Home

*British Royal Guards. Taken at Windsor Castle*

Sunday the 17th November 1974. The Australis docked at midday in Southampton, but I didn't disembark until 5 o'clock that evening. My uncle was collecting me, and it had been arranged that I would stay with him until I found other lodgings. He lived in Mitcham, Surrey and I remembered the old house had a pebbledash effect on the outside.

My early childhood memories of that home remained fresh in my mind. I remember family Christmases with all the other grandchildren sitting together at trestle tables, aunts and uncles, mum and dad and of course Nan who wore an apron serving up the Christmas lunch and Grandad who always wanted to say a long winded speech before we were allowed down from the table and ripping into our presents.

I thought I'd feel comfortable and safe there with its little rooms and my uncle who was renowned for his cheeky sense of humour. (Huh!) Instead there was a distinct feeling of not being wanted or intruding or something.

There was nothing I could do about it for the time being anyway. After we dropped Alan off at his house it was a silent trip to Ray's. The house seemed smaller somehow and it was cold and maybe even damp an uncomfortable feeling was creeping up on me. I was given a bedroom and told not to go snooping and never go into 'that' room, it was locked anyway...I tried the door when he wasn't looking.

A couple of days later Ray and I were going to get my suitcase but as there was a rail strike the roads were too busy, so we went into London sightseeing instead. The London Underground Tube trains were all working, and he showed me how to buy tickets and read the maps. Maybe my thoughts about Ray were unfounded because we had a wonderful day together and he even took me shopping so I could buy some clothes, I really needed my suitcase.

I'd been given a letter of introduction to the manager of a German Delicatessen in Soho, called **Schmidt's'**. The sales representative who came to the shop where I worked in Australia was a personal friend of Mr. Heinz Keller, the man I wanted to see but unfortunately, he wasn't there. However not all was lost because I was given a phone number and told to ring the next day.

The next important destination was the NSW bank. I needed to know if my transferred money had arrived. Ray took me on a walking tour of London, and not only did we find the bank I was assured the money was safely deposited. This was my safety net but at that present time I still had plenty of travelers cheques to tide me over, so they got exchanged for Pounds sterling.

It gets dark very early in November, so we decided to head back to Mitcham. I was entertained on the train journey home and kept getting the giggles because Ray was People Watching. He whispered all sorts of rude comments about them or made up stories of what they did in life. It was very hard not to make eye contact with his victims, but he kept telling me to turn and look at someone or another or even check them out through the reflections in the windows when we were in the dark tunnels.

The train strike was the over the next day and eventually got to Southampton to collect my suitcase. What a relief!

I also rang Mr. Keller and was asked to come and meet him. So, with my new found knowledge of the London underground transport system and retracing my steps back to Schmidt's with reference letter in hand I got the job. Told to start Monday. They would have preferred if I could speak German but that can't be helped. The job provides all my meals for free and I would be expected to work all different shifts. I forgot to ask how much my wages would be because I was so happy to have done this all by myself all in one day. Ray said he'd help me sort out my working cards, whatever they are.

*Chapter 6*

# Mum's Clan

## The Explanation

*Mum's relatives quite a few years ago
at the wedding of my cousin Janet to Howard*

Uncle John is the eldest, Mum is tucked in the middle and 4 years her junior is Gina. All now married with offspring of their own.

Mum's mum also known as Nan loves a bit of a drink and her live in lover was Uncle Peter, an Irish man with a strong accent who manages to pop a 'fuck" or "bastard" into every sentence without even the slightest hint of malice and has giant wandering hands that take pleasure in seeking out any unsuspecting female's boobs. Nan has a sister, Great Aunty Ethel and they absolutely loath each other.

Aunty Ethel is a polished person with high morals and never a drop of the hard stuff passes her lips, a hard-working husband who I call Uncle Tom and my second cousin David, their son. I'll tell you a little about him later.

Not forgetting Great Gran Spriggs who is the mother of Nan and Aunt Ethel and has a penchant to Guinness because she says she needs the iron and is cared for by the Tea-Totaler.

These all live in England except for mum of course. Gina with her family tried to live the Australian way for six long years but she had to scuttle back home because calling a bank manager by his first name was just too hard to bear.

*Back to my story again.*

*Chapter 7*

# England Part Two
## Greeted With A Smile

*A Pub in Epsom, Surrey, England*

I'd written to my mum's brother, John, and he and his wife invited me up on Saturday. Ray explained how to catch the three different trains I needed to get to St Albans and John was there to meet me.

This time we recognized each other instantly. He looked exactly as I remembered him, and he said I had the same nose as my mum. Besides, not many of us got off the train. Betty, John's wife, gave me a warm welcome and their new puppy, called Blacky, (guess what colour she is) wriggled and weed in total excitement. What a greeting.

I was taken to the shops and we met up with my cousin Janet and her little boy called Howard, she speaks with a really horrible accent and instead of Howard, it *Arrrd'* and to make matters worse, her husband has the same name and they shout a lot.

Asked if I wanted to spend the night with them or go to a dance with John and Betty. I chose the dance. It was so much fun especially when John, his two friends and I donned some scrappy black wigs and sang Beatles songs.

There is no hot water at John's old house. The open fire has to be lit and the pipes that run up behind it heat the water. Thank god its wintertime or it would be a cold bath. That's another thing, no shower. I suppose if that's the way you normally live you get used to it, but I found it quite strange.

Sunday morning John took me to an antique fair that was out in an open field, which was freezing and boggy. We didn't buy anything but getting to know him was interesting. I found out that he has a great interest in anything ancient and showed me where there are remains of Roman walls and roads all around the area.

I remember as a child when my family came to visit, there was countryside surrounded by fields and little tracks with wooden styles you climbed over. Janet and I would go into the hedge rows and look for bird's nests with eggs in them.

Now there are houses everywhere.

Lunch was at Janet's beautiful old house with a brook down the bottom of the garden. It would be so peaceful if they just talked normally and not yell all the time.

Mind you, everyone made me so welcome and when it was time to head back to Mitcham, John gave me an envelope and said not to open it until I got on the train. Inside was a crisp ten-pound note plus a letter saying that I was welcome to stay anytime.

## *Chapter 8*
# **Fr. Schmidt**
## The Old German Delicatessen

*An old photo of Schmidt's deli.*
*Unfortunately I didn't take a photograph of this place*
*and now it no longer exists*

Monday, new job, butterflies in my stomach. Would I remember how to get there? Well I did and although the work wasn't hard it just seemed a strange place. The building was in the Fitzrovia district of Soho, a German area and it still had a 1920's feel about the place.

Apparently, it had to close during the war for obvious reasons and they had a notice on the window stating that their son was also in the army...but which one?

There were many floors all accessible by an elevator. The top floor was where staff were given a cooked meal, the levels just below were the food preparation and kitchens for the shop and restaurant, all food was served on metal platters. One below that was a restaurant which was full of German people eating German food. Usually plenty of red cabbage and Wursts with mustard. Ground level was the delicatessen with beautiful tins of European goodies plus meats and cheeses the kinds I'd never seen or heard of before.

This is where you ordered and paid for your meal. Below ground level was the storeroom but one day I went down even further by accident and it was so creepy. Men who were pale with translucent skin and looked like they hadn't seen sunshine or even the outside world before appeared and ogled me. I felt danger instantly and quickly got back in the lift and bashed the buttons. Relief when the doors closed, and I was back in the shop.

One of the other older shop assistance looked at me and guessed what had happened. She said, "NEVER go down there, they will hurt you if they get hold of you". What was this place? I think that's where they made the Wurst sausages, possibly from lost people.

The waiters from the restaurant, noted for their surly grumpiness, would come into the shop and flick tea towels. Everyone would yell at them and send them scurrying back upstairs. Apparently, they were stealing. The towel would flick and catch a packet of biscuits or whatever they aimed at and they would artfully catch and hide the goods in their waistcoats.

Once a customer only left a small tip, which they placed under a saucer, hoping to get away before the small offering was noticed but to their dismay the waiter with an expert flick of his towel sent the offending sixpence flying after them and saying with great contempt,

*"You sink ve are SLAVES?!*

My work hours were long and varied. Sometimes I had to start very early in the morning and leave in the evening, other times I started about lunchtime and didn't leave until about eleven at night and then make a dash for the train, so I didn't miss the last connecting one back to Colliers Wood Station.

That's also when I found out that Soho was the equivalent to Sydney's Kings Cross.

During the day the strip clubs and adult book shops simply blended in but at night it was a different atmosphere altogether. Scantily dressed women, (even in winter??) Men spruiking from shop fronts enticing other men (or women) into their establishments for pleasures beyond their wildest imaginations. People walking around, checking everyone else out. It was actually exciting, and I never felt scared. Busy, full of colour with laughter, drunks and cheeky wisecracks the place felt alive.

Getting off the train in Mitcham at around midnight meant a walk through the common to get home. One night a policeman in a Panda car called me over and asked what I was doing.

I told him I'd just finished work in London and going home. He didn't like me walking by myself at that time of night so gave me a lift.

He wanted to know when I'd be doing that same shift again, so I told him and although I think he wasn't supposed to, he collected me and took me home safely each night.

## Chapter 9
# Meeting Up Again
## A Timely Move

*Uncle Peter, Nan, Doreen and I. In a pub in Ealing*

One Wednesday on my day off I met up with Doreen, and I must admit that I'd missed her and Alwyn these last couple of weeks, we had built quite a good friendship and now had a lot in common so plenty of shared experiences to talk about. She looked dejected.

To brighten the mood, we took ourselves off sightseeing. Hyde Park is beautiful in the winter and as we were wrapped up warmly, walking through the city was lovely. I think she had broken up with Keith who she'd met on the ship, he had helped her find a flat and a job, but the relationship didn't last once he got back home with his family and friends.

Life's like that unfortunately, not the same carefree madness that we'd grown accustom to in those heady weeks at sea.

As I was going to visit Nan on Saturday, I suggested that Doreen could come along as well. She liked that idea and we arranged to meet at Waterloo Station by the book shop at 10AM. before travelling together on the Central Line tube to Ealing Broadway.

When I was little, we lived in Ealing in a house that had 3 bedrooms, a garden out the back and a beautiful cherry tree that I loved to climb. Nan would visit us most days. I also liked visiting her.

She and Uncle Peter lived in the room below ground level of a terrace house. The kitchen table was pushed up against the window and you could watch the people's legs and feet as they walked by. It really was only one room because their bed was in there as well, the divider wall gave her a small kitchen with a cooker and sink.

The toilet and bathroom were shared with whoever lived in the top floors of this house and she had to go upstairs for that. As a child, I never thought about other people's living conditions but now I was beginning to understand why my dad wanted to migrate to Australia in the first place. Was this really a comfortable way to live?

Nan had prepared a meal for us before we headed over to one of her local pubs to meet Uncle Peter. Nan and Peter have a lot of local pubs I was yet to discover.

She would always start with half a pint of Lager with a splash of lime cordial, Peter had a shot of whiskey and then went to another pub called 'The Rose & Crown' where everyone seemed to be knocking back quite a few pints. Nan was now on the straight Gin with one cube of ice and Uncle Peter downed many, many pints. Nan seemed to accept it as normal.

The same when Uncle Peter's hands started their usual exploration adventures and the language got fruitier, so we just laughed nervously along. Doreen thought it was all a bit strange, it was really, I would have warned her if I'd known.

Luckily the pubs close mid-afternoon so that's when we said goodbye.

I wanted to see our old house at number 6 Overdale Road and Mrs. Graphan the next-door neighbour.

Just as we were about to knock on her door out, she came with hat and coat on, the timing was wrong. (I wonder if she thought we were Jehovah's Witnesses?) She gave me a hug and told me to write to her and let her know the next time because she'd love to see me.

Mrs. Graphan's daughter's name was also Jenny but she was a teenager when I was a little girl and now married and moved away. Funny the silly things you remember, Jenny used to always give me the plastic toys out of the cornflakes packet. I'd climb the fence and she'd pass them over to me.

There were more memories I wanted to revisit in Ealing, but it was getting dark and cold. Neither of us wanted to go back home yet so on the spur of the moment we decided to find a bed and breakfast place nearby and continue the exploration the next day.

Believe it or not, we found just the place and a delightful lady greeted us. Breakfast next morning was huge and delicious and not expensive. All set, we went to Ganersbury Park and even played on the swings, walked up to my old school, crossing the railway bridge with the railings that I got my head stuck in when I was little (I was a mischievous urchin). It is all part of the underground railway but by the time you get to Ealing you're in daylight not tunnels any more.

Things had changed and of course looked so much smaller. The corner shop where I would spend my one shilling weekly pocket money, one halfpenny at a time was now a house. Obviously, my purchases paid off for the owner. Our street was no longer a steep hill but merely a slight incline and number 6 looked shabby.

Time for Doreen and I to go our separate ways but not until we got to Wembley Station. Doreen was telling me about her flat in Leasvsdon with a spare room, I was interested.

Instead of heading back to Mitcham we went together to Watford and then we caught a bus. Her flat was fabulous. It was actually a 3-story townhouse owned by a fellow called Phil. He was at home when we got there, and I asked if I could move in as well.

Not a problem and if we shared a room, we could halve the rent. Shared a room with Doreen that is, not with him. Perfect, the room had 2 single beds and everything we needed, sheets, towels, all the kitchen gadgets, the lot. Even better, Phil hardly ever stayed, he lived with his girlfriend most of the time.

I couldn't get back to Mitcham quick enough to tell Ray about my good luck. I also decided to give the Schmidt's job away as it was too far to travel, and the wages were rubbish as well as the hours. I'm sure I'd find something else soon enough and I still had money in the NSW bank that I hadn't touched yet. I don't know who was happier, him or me? Ray that is.

Once I'd moved in with Doreen, I found that work wasn't quite as easy to find as I thought it would be. Still not fussed though.

It was time to visit Mum's aunt in Cheshire for a weekend. I loved the train travel even if it meant changing at different stations, all part of the adventure. Aunty Ethel lived in a quaint little village called Alderley Edge.

As I'd left really early in the morning from home, it was only about lunchtime when I got there. My suitcase was still the same old red one that I had when I travelled to Ayres Rock two years before and although I didn't have much in it, the handle would dig into my hand if I carried it too far.

The station master was in his cute little hut at Alderley Edge station so I asked if I could leave the suitcase there and collect it later. He assured me that Aunty Ethel didn't live far away (everyone knows each other in these small villages) but I wanted to find that out for myself. He was telling the truth, so once all the hellos and have a cup of tea and a giant slice of homemade cake and don't you look like your mother niceties were over, I walked back and collected it.

Great Gran Spriggs lived with Aunty Ethel, Uncle Tom and mum's cousin David and she was very old and fragile. Because of this Aunty Ethel had to give up work to look after her. Aunty Ethel had worked for the Ferranti family since she was a girl. She was employed as a companion to the daughter and stayed on as housekeeper come everything else all these years later. In truth, she was the friend to this wealthy family who lived in a Henbury Hall.

In fact, so special to them that in their Will they had an arrangement. She would receive an amount of money every year until she died. (Aunty Ethel died aged 94 by the way) Uncle Tom still went out to work as an engineer and David worked on the railways.

I later found out that David was autistic. At the time I just thought he was a pain in the bum.

The countryside in Cheshire is beautiful. They took me for a scenic drive. I was given the little room at the front of the house and a wedding photo of my mum and dad hung on the wall.

A funny contraption that woke me up in the morning and made me a cup of tea called a **Teasmaid** had been set up. I didn't like to let on that I don't drink tea so I downed as much as I could quickly before getting up and ready for the day.

The family had a very fat little Beagle dog called Max which I took for a walk, but we couldn't go too far as the poor thing puffed and panted and I was worried that it might collapse and die.

David (who was in the same shape as the dog) took me for a tour of Manchester, and then to the pictures.

This was most embarrassing because David has no social skills at all. God I thought I was bad enough!!

You were allowed to smoke in the pictures back then. David had a pipe and proceeded to empty the bowl into a metal ashtray that was fixed to the seats in front.

Emptying a pipe means knocking out the contents, so here he was bashing his pipe inches away from the person in fronts head then refilling, lighting and puffing away only to repeat the whole performance about fifteen minutes later.

As well he'd bought a huge packet of individually wrapped sweets with the shiny noisy paper reaching 120 decibels per sweet which he rustled and munched on through the whole film.

I'm surprised people only gave him filthy looks and not a punch in the head. I was so happy to get out of there.

After an amazingly comfortable warm sleep it was time to say my goodbyes and head for home. Only this time I couldn't pick up my suitcase. Aunty Ethel had filled it up with jams, preserves, an apple pie, eggs, apples a new diary and a rain hat. Then she gave me ten pounds to cover the cost of my fare home.

I accepted the goodies even though I wondered how the hell I was going to carry everything, shame wheels on suitcases weren't invented yet. But I refused the money, which was a waste of time because she said it was my Christmas present and it would be rude to refuse.

Luckily, I was given a lift to the station and with herculean effort I got all the way plus up the stairs home without bursting a Foofa Valve.

Doreen worked at Woolworths in Watford and she was now going out with one of the managers named Denis. He was nice enough and they didn't mind me tagging along when they headed out for a walk along the beautiful canal near where we lived.

Christmas was fast approaching, and we needed decorations for the flat.

Perfect, I spied a Holly tree, but the best branches were up high.

Not to worry, I climbed and broke off branches whilst they were the lookouts. It was a painful process and but worth it, the scars have healed.

A letter arrived from Stewart the Scottish guy from the Australis reminding us of the invitation to his place for Hogmanay. That put paid to my job searching, I'd look for something later when we got back.

Christmas Eve was spent at The New Penny Disco where I met Glen and his friend John. Denis was getting tired of dancing, but Doreen and I seemed to have enough energy for everyone, so Glen and John took over.

We danced until two in the morning when it was chuck out time, besides there's only so much **Wombling Merry Christmas** you can put up with. Glen drove us all back to our flat where we continued playing records until everyone eventually flaked out.

Glen and John went home about 10am and Denis stayed on whilst we made Christmas lunch then he went about 7.30pm.

Boxing Day didn't exist until mid-afternoon. Glen and John turned up again and took us out to a pub where we played snooker. They were so much fun.

Glen did karate, played football and boxed, a super fit good-looking guy but I never found out what work he did. John was an engineer who also had a portable disco and did weddings and parties. His wit was fast and funny. Denis seemed to have disappeared.

Living in Leavsdon was great. We weren't too far from meandering canals with beautiful but sometimes grumpy swans and ducks, long canal boats and lochs also deep dark woods with jumpy squirrels not too far away.

There were cottages and at one place we saw a donkey, so I climbed the fence to give it a pat. The canal paths weren't always easy, some areas they had been maintained but others just a boggy muddy track, didn't matter, we'd be dressed in jeans, coats, gloves, boots and hats so we didn't care.

Often, we'd walk for miles, sometimes ending up in Rickmansworth other times in Hemel Hempstead and forgetting we were hungry until we came upon a village where we'd stop and buy an apple or an ice-cream to sustain us.

Heading home we'd look for road signs to Watford or Leavsdon or somewhere that we knew. Sometimes we'd catch a bus back another time we'd hitch a ride and other times we'd just walk and call in to the local fish and chip shop for take away dinner.

Speaking of Fish and Chips, that's what I called Glen. *My Fish & Chips Guy.* He only ever turned up on a Friday, stayed until Sunday and then disappeared again. Found out later that he was a married man with a wife who didn't understand him.... Poor baby....I wonder what line he gave her when he buggered off every weekend.

# Chapter 10
# Hogmany
## 1975

*Doreen, Stewart, Me and Alwyn. One of the places we celebrated*
*Hogmanay in Scotland. We three girls are still friends to this day.*
*Unfortunately we never kept in touch with Stewart.*

Doreen was back at work on the Monday, so I bought our coach tickets to Edinburgh. Bright and early Tuesday morning, we caught a bus, a train, a tube and finally a coach then arrived in Bonny Scotland 9 hours later to be met by Alwyn and Stewart.

Clambering into Stewart's cousin's taxi and headed for his family home in Dunfermline. We made it! What a crowd! Stewart's mum and dad were brilliant. They made up makeshift beds all over the house for all of us. We were fed and then got changed into glad rags and headed out for a dance.

I could hardly understand anyone, their accents were so strong, but it didn't matter we all had fun anyway. I even joined in with a darts match. That same night we went back to Stewart's, changed into our more comfortable jeans and headed out again getting ready for "The Bells" which is the start of Hogmanay.

Having the darkest hair, I was chosen to be the **First Footer**. Stewart's dad had given me a lump of coal, Black Bun and some shortbread to take to the first house. I wasn't sure what all the tradition was all about but just went along with it.

Everyone was given a shot of Whiskey and the celebrations began. Six houses later each with a gram of whiskey to wet your whistle. I didn't have any feeling left in my hands and feet. Funny enough though, the whiskey was horrible, but I wasn't drunk or cold.

Finally arriving back at Stewart's about 10.30am we all crashed until the afternoon. Stewart's mum fed us before we headed out again to more parties. This time we got back earlier, about 5.30am.

When we finally surfaced, we all went for a walk around Dunfermline. It is a town full of history, in fact it was once the capital of Scotland. A former Royal Burgh and parish in Fife and only 5 km from the Firth of Forth.

The 12th century Abbey is the final resting place of Robert the Bruce as well as 11 Kings and Queens. King Malcolm Canmore established his court after the death of Macbeth...I thought Macbeth was just a story made up by Shakespeare.

The next day Doreen, Stewart, Alwyn and I headed into Edinburgh. Somehow, we managed to lose Alwyn and Stewart, but Doreen and I didn't mind, we climbed the rock to the castle, but it was all locked up. What a shame, but the view from up there was magic.

We had lunch and noticed Haggis was on the menu but neither of us was game enough to give it a try. There was a police box that looked just like the Tardis, so I called in "Dr Who' and to my great shock out came a policeman and asked me what I was doing. He'd never heard of Dr Who and said he'd have to look out for it.

Bobby the little statue of a faithful dog was sitting out there in the cold and it made me sad. We bought a load of souvenirs and some presents for Stewart's family then found the train station and made our way back to their house.

It was time to go home, we said our goodbyes and Stewart had a friend heading our way, so we got a ride and he dropped us off near an inn about lunchtime.

From there we hitch hiked and managed to get a lift all the way into London. That night we stayed at Doreen's cousin's flat where a group of friends were having a marathon card game.

I crashed on a chair and Doreen crashed on a settee. About 4am we were woken up by people moving mattresses into the living room and we were given sleeping bags which were a lot more comfortable than curled up in a foetal position.

God knows what time everyone surfaced the next day, but I remember that breakfast was Pizza and beer washed down with rough red wine in the Pizza Parlour down the road. After that Doreen and I managed somehow to make it all the way home.

Whilst all this madness and mayhem was going on in our lives, the news from Australia seemed like they were having madness and mayhem of a more serious kind.

Darwin had been completely flattened by Cyclone Tracy a category 5 cyclone on Christmas day and 71 people were killed. The navy ship HMAS Brisbane arrived by New Year's Day, the army was sent in and many people helped in the clean-up.

My mum was one of the people who manned the phones meanwhile England was selling records for the Darwin appeal.

The Chandris ship the SS Patris was commissioned by the Australian government to become emergency accommodation for 5500 people until November 1975.

If that wasn't bad enough down the other end of the country a bulk ore carrying ship called **Lake Illawarra** travelling up the Derwent River hit the pylons of the Tasman Bridge.

The bridge then collapsed taking cars and people with it before the ship sank over the top of them. Five occupants of four cars and seven crew of the ship died on that day.

One car, a Monaro owned by Frank Manley was teetering on the edge of the collapsed bridge, he, his wife, the brother in law and daughter were in the car and some miraculous way they managed to climb out. There was another car next to them that was in the same terrifying position.

What a horrible start to the year but as I was a mere 20-year-old and far away from home this news didn't impact on me for weeks, not until I received letters from home telling me of these disasters.

# Chapter 11
# **Back to Reality**
## of Sorts

*Doreen and I mucking around
on the canal near where we lived.*

Back to the business of job hunting once we returned from the land of the Scots. I applied for a receptionist job. Didn't get it. Marks & Spence's shop assistant job. Didn't get it. Woolworth's. Got it. Probably because Doreen put in a good word for me.

We were to work one Saturday a fortnight as well as Monday to Friday and then had a rostered day off. In England the main meal of the day is usually lunch time and many places either provide lunch for free or a cheap rate. This is what we had in Woolworth's. For just 10p you got a full lunch plus dessert and a cup of tea or coffee, so we decided to go along with that and just have a snack for dinner. The snack was usually a healthy bar of chocolate or ice-cream and as for breakfast...who needed that anyway?

They were kind enough to let Doreen and I have the same working days so our days off were always together and we spent them sightseeing in London mainly. Mum and Dad were thinking of coming to England for the first time since they immigrated but Dad couldn't find his birth certificate and needed it for a passport. That gave us a good excuse to go to Summerset House and rummage through old registrar books.

It took a while to find Dad's registration of existence. He was born on 14th November 1924 but wasn't in the old handwritten book until March 1925. I was told that the parents had 41 days to register a birth and the books were only updated quarterly. No wonder it took so long for me to find him.

After all that I took Doreen to Schmidt's to show her the place where I'd worked. Rose, one of the shop assistance told me to buy something. I said we'd both have a coffee and a loaf of bread but instead we not only got our coffee and bread, we came away with 6 little cakes, one large cake and 4 bars of chocolate all for 26p. Guilty pleasures.

Another time in London we met 2 Central American guys who came for England to improve their English. One was to be a policeman and the other was studying chemistry.

It was our turn to be tour guides and we had a great day. We both decided that we loved England as there was always so much to see and do. Although I should have been more careful with my spelling when I wrote home and said I was RAPED instead of RAPT when I told my parents of an exciting adventure. They were nearly on the next plane out until mum calmed down and continued reading and of course realizing my normal dreadful spelling.

I had a letter from Nick, my boyfriend who worked on the Australis. He'd met Mum and Dad in Melbourne and was on his way back to Southampton in February. He asked if I would be there to meet him?

Well, of course I would be. I'd have to arrange my workdays off, but I was sure that could happen.

Tuesday 4th February the Australis made its way into Southampton docks and Doreen and I were there to meet it.

Other girls were there as well to meet their old beaus plus I met a guy who'd come to meet his girlfriend.

Once they could disembark, we hailed a taxi and headed into the town to a Greek restaurant and then shopping. Later we snuck back on board and met up with a whole lot of other crew members who remembered us.

Lots of hugs and kisses and also Nick showed me the table in the Pacific dining room where he served my Mum and Dad lunch when they visited him in Melbourne.

Later everyone took off to a Greek nightclub where we Zorba danced the night away before sneaking back on board about 4am. Doreen and I stayed tucked up and hidden when the guys had lifeboat drill before we all went ashore again. Leaving at 2.30pm and resisting the pleas from Nick to make me stow away with him.

No matter where we went fun seemed to find us. Even bringing the shopping home one day with an extra heavy load I stopped for a breather when a policeman called over and asked if I was OK?

I said yes, but cheekily said he could give me a lift home if he wanted to. He laughed and said he would have if he had a car, then noticed the bag of crisps and asked if I was going to have a party and could he come. I said sure, he could look after us. His answer to that was "Hell no, I'd come to enjoy myself, *wink wink*" With that the bus arrived and the bus driver was just as cheeky.

The buses don't run too often between Leavsdon and Watford and if you miss it, it's about an hour to wait for the next one. The nights draw in quickly wintertime and I'd just missed the bus so decided to walk home rather than wait about and freeze to death.

It was dark and cold, but I'd warm up with the walk. I was wrapped up in my duffle coat and scarf.

Part of the journey home was past the Leavsdon airport and the fog was descending. It got thicker and thicker until I couldn't even see my own hands in front of my face.

Footsteps were echoing and I thought I was being followed but couldn't see anyone.

As I began to walk faster and then start running with my hand brushing up against the fence as a guide all of a sudden, my scarf was yanked backwards and me with it.

I couldn't even scream through terror and being choked.

I realized my scarf had caught on the fence and fish hooked me. Never in my life have I been that scared.

## Chapter 12

# To Move or Not to Move

## That is the Question

*Doreen and I in our flat in Leavsden*

Doreen and I were getting itchy feet and work was uninspiring. She had two invitations to come for a visit from distant relatives who she'd never met, so she asked if I could go as well. What could they say?

We both handed our notice in to Woolworths and hoped we could find jobs when we got back. Phil our landlord had a friend called Frank who wanted to move in so he took over our rent but said we could keep our stuff there and we'd work something out when we got back. Easy.

Off to Liverpool. We spent one night back in London at the cousin's house then an early morning dash to Victoria Station where we caught the coach to Liverpool.

I liked coach journey's you get to see a lot of the country and if it's a long trip they stop off at eating places along the way so we can refuel. Once we reached Liverpool, we asked the way to the Fazakerley and took the local bus. Then we went into a garage and asked for Drake Street, so the guy gave us a lift in a chauffer's car.

It pays to be a young 20-year-old girl sometimes. Aunty May and Uncle Bill were a wonderful old couple who welcomed us with open arms.

Uncle Bill and I became expert paper plane throwers and Aunty May took us to church meetings. We also indulged every evening with a 99 from the Mr Whippy van.

As the Lake District is only about 100 miles away, we headed there by bus and stopped at a beautiful town called Kendal. On the bus we met two Moroccan guys who now lived nearby and knew the area. They took us to a pub called The Golden Lion where we booked in for the night. We met up with them again later and had dinner at the Labour Club, played darts and had a dance then walked back to the Golden Lion on the icy streets late at night.

The owner of the pub had left the door on the latch for us and our room was lovely and warm. Next morning when we looked out the window, it had been snowing and the Golden Lion statue looked rather chilly.

We took our time exploring Kendal and found a ruined castle that belonged to one of Henry the 8th's wives. It was only a quick postcard visit with the return trip back to Liverpool already booked for the following day. We again enjoyed the scenery but didn't meet any dishy guys that time.

Just one more night in Liverpool before heading back to Leavsdon and then over to Western Supermare. This time it was Doreen's cousin John. He lived in a bungalow and is a bachelor who has a sometimes live in girlfriend. She obviously didn't mind him having two 20-year-old girls come and stay, unless he didn't tell her.

He was great, he took us sightseeing around WSM and it has a huge sandy beach. The tide goes out for miles and leaves little boats stranded all along the shore. It was far too cold for beach weather, but it would be brilliant in the summer I imagine.

Then we headed to Wells, which is in Summerset and is the smallest city in England. They have a magnificent cathedral and also Bishop's Place where wild swans go and ring a bell when they want to be fed.

We had lunch at an old-fashioned pub before heading to Cheddar and walked up the gorge. The road winds its way with massive rocks leering over you. Apparently, the boulders in Cheddar Gorge manage to kill at least one person a year or at least flatten a car, maybe time to do something about that I think. We trod very warily.

A place called the '**Wookey Hole** was another place we visited which is a cave in a series of limestone caverns about 60,000 years old, at the southern edge of the Mendip Hills.

Cheddar is famous for its cheese and we heard the ice cream wasn't bad either. Taste testing time was on the agenda and I must admit that the ice-cream we had was creamy yellow in colour and the most delicious one I have ever had. Nothing has ever matched it.

Just to creep us out we went to an old disused mill with ancient playground toys dating back to 1896 and a storage area for unwanted Madame Tussauds Wax models. Nightmare material. It only needed discordant music to send shivers down my spine.

John had to get back to work and we had to get back to something, but at that stage, we had no idea what was around the next corner.

The Leavsdon flat had another bedroom on the ground floor and we managed to talk Frank into moving down there so we could have our old bedroom back.

Job hunting started in earnest once again. We both went for waitressing jobs in London but on arrival we didn't fancy it. Saw an interesting position for people to meet Americans...hmm...only to find out it was selling pots and pans.

Not quite what we expected but then again, we didn't know what to expect.

Train rides back and forth to the big smoke were always fun and tinged with the unexpected. One time a group of French football fans crowded out the whole carriage. One guy offered me a seat...on his lap, others all wanted kisses. Doreen wasn't amused but I was. WOW a whole carriage full of gorgeousness with very sexy accents; *Be still my beating heart.*

Another time it was Birmingham football fans and they were even harder to understand than the frogs. Just as much fun though and we all went to the pub together.

Occasionally we nipped into Schmidt's for a cheap lunch to sustain us in our seemed like never ending job rejections. Then finally one day I applied for a barmaid job at The Crown in Watford and actually got it. The only form of ID I had with me at the time was a letter from Mum, addressed to: "Little Jenny Wert, from your dopey mother"

Mr Bingley, the boss just laughed and said that would do. It wasn't a live-in job but only about 25 minutes away from the flat, so I'd be staying for a while.

Doreen wasn't so lucky with a barmaid job at another local pub but soon got a live-in position where she decided to try out nursing. It meant our coexistence was coming to an end.

We peeled off posters from the bedroom walls and re stuck the wallpaper that came with them with nail polish...*Shhh.* Frank offered to drive Doreen to her cousin's house before she embarked on her new career. I went along for the ride.

Frank had an MG which really only had 2 seats, but we managed to get us all in plus Doreen's huge suitcases and as it was still very cold, the hood was up. He also suggested a sightseeing tour of London which was a difficult and squishy way of seeing the old town.

Red double decker buses loomed over us, Black cabs whizzed around knowingly, and we craned our necks and shuffled around in that miniature car until we both felt very car sick and begged him to stop.

It was fun though and I remember a couple of stupid songs on the radio as we were zooming around. One was about an over aged Groupie named Jenny. What cheek, pinching my name in vain. It was called Queen of 1964" by Neil Sedaka.

The other stupid song was Bulldog drinks champagne. By Jim Stafford'. Good Honky-tonk stuff to drive by.

*Chapter 13*

# The Crown

## Pulling Pints

*A Pub that looked like the Crown.*
*The Crown now has a different name and facade.*
*This photo is like the one I worked in.*

Now a respectable working woman, well sort of. I worked 48 hours a week over 10 sessions. The mornings were in the Public bar and I generally wore jeans and very casual clothes.

The customers were just one level up from Scumbags but hilariously funny. I got quite good at pouring the odd pints from the five different beers on tap. I soon got to remember the locals favourite concoctions and could even scroll my name, or something rude into the froth of a Guinness whilst pouring.

The evenings were in the Saloon bar, dressed in more respectable attire we quite often had the same cheeky customers but this time well behaved and mannered because they were accompanied with their wives. Many a time I blackmailed them in the morning sessions.

The pubs used to close mid-afternoon and reopen again around 6.30pm. Instead of the walk home and back again I'd stay and be given lunch by the chefs in the restaurant which was part of the pub.

Tony, a barman, who lived at the pub, had jet black hair, which was purchased from the chemist, the jet-black bit, not the hair. With my minimal hairdressing experience, I was able to dye it for him in our free time when the regrowth started to show. I had my uses.

Going home at night one of the customers would often give me a lift but if they'd had too much of the hard stuff, John the other barman would do the honours.

A lot of the regulars were bus drivers or conductors from the nearby bus station, sometimes on my way to work a giant green double decker bus would pull over and I'd get a personally chauffeured lift to work. The bus would be on the way back to the depot so empty of passengers.

This is where I met Bill. He was a bus driver. Young, not bad looking, with long dark brown hair, moustache and twinkly eyes.

After the evening shift we'd go to Bailies" the disco and meet up with his friends. Sometimes the local Chew & Spew' which was our name for the Chinese restaurant. If I'd finished work in the afternoon and didn't have an evening shift we'd quite often go to another pub and meet up with his brother, Bob and his girlfriend Mary.

I'd be invited along to the Bus Drivers & Engineers dance but always preferred to walk home after that because they all got a bit too Pie Eyed. God knows how they sobered up enough to take controls of the buses the next day.

Weekends that I wasn't working Bill, Bob, Mary and I would head into the countryside. We went to Windsor Castle and watched changing of the guards, Bill bought me a monkey from the souvenir shop, and I called it Funky Gibbon after the Goodies song that was the played on the radio all the time.

We'd go to lovely little country pubs and even boat rides on the Thames. A favourite place was the Bier Keller, a German beer garden. They had a German Oompah-pah band, and wear German national dress and slap each other around with their dance routines. Good fun.

On a long weekend we drove from North Wales down to South Wales in two days. We slept in the car and to the dismay of a local shop keeper, we bought a loaf of bread and a chunk of cheese which we ripped and tore into like savages whilst sitting in the car park. He said he would have loaned us a knife if we'd only asked.

A sweet old customer at The Crown named George was in a bit of a dither one day. His wife was in America visiting relatives and whilst she was away, George was supposed to be redecorating their house.

Well, he'd spent most of his waking hours at The Crown and now WH Day was fast approaching...Panic!! (Wife Home Day) So a Posse of customers and Crown staff (including me) gathered at his house during the mid-afternoon closing times and not only got the job done but tidied up as well.

### Hooray!

Good old George was so grateful. He bought round after round for everyone but as I don't drink, I got the best gift. A whole box of Mars Bars, 36 in all. I think I got through them in just eleven days. Brilliant....and a bit sickening.... but hey, they were Mars bars!

Work was fun but the pay was a lousy, seventeen pounds a week once tax came out. That old *Itchy Feet Syndrome* was setting in again. I was also getting rather sick of winter. Biting the bullet, I handed in my notice. Also, I'd caught a cold and felt miserable.

I rang Aunty Ethel and asked if I could come up and stay for a couple of weeks just to sort my head out. I'd also decided to leave the flat, Phil hardly ever came home, and I think Frank thought I was there just to tidy up after him. Bugger that! Anyway, she said yes.

Then I asked Uncle John if I could plonk my excess belongings at his house and the answer was yes again.

Bill drove me to Uncle John's and was going to drive me up to Alderley Edge in Cheshire until he realised how far away it was. I was secretly pleased actually because I knew she wouldn't have approved of him. Instead he drove me to the station.

Would you believe it? On the train I saw an old poster for Jersey.

It said: ***Escape the winter blues. Come for the sunshine.***

I didn't even know where Jersey was, but I was already sold.

When I arrived at Aunty Ethel's she wasn't as pleased to see me this time. She grumblingly said I was more like her sister. Oh boy, rules and etiquette; you've just got to get them correct.

An Australian upbringing is not quite 'Tea and scones' like she is used to I'm afraid. It might have also been the fact that she had a rotten cold and Gran Spriggs had the trots so badly that the whole house reeked of it.

I made myself useful in the cup of tea making and then found an old garden bench that needed sprucing up with a scrub and paint job. Still she knew where Jersey was and thought it was a wonderful idea that I buggered off there. A couple of days later my passage had been booked.

David drove me to Knutsford where I caught a 9.42am bus, waited there for three quarters of an hour then another bus to Cheltenham, waited again and yet another bus to Weymouth.

Finally arriving about 8.30pm and after finding the ferry terminal and purchasing my ticket for the midnight trip I hunted out somewhere warm and comfortable to sit out the last few hours of the evening.

Getting close to the launch time I went wandering towards the terminus when I saw a bloke trip and fall heavily on the pavement. I raced over to him and he'd knocked himself out. I yelled for help until a window of the house I happened to be outside, opened and told them to ring for an ambulance.

When the ambulance arrived, they told me my fallen man was just drunk. With that he woke up and told whoever would listen that I saved him, and he wanted to marry me. YIKES! Get me out of there, besides I had a ferry to catch.

## *Chapter 14*
# Jersey
## The Promise of Sunshine

*A postcard from Jersey*

I must have dozed off on the ferry because at one time announcements were blaring out about arriving in Guernsey then probably about an hour later the announcements were for Jersey. The sun was just coming up and it was 6am. Blearily I walked that great long pier and eventually made it to the foot path.

Now what?

I asked some of the other passengers about the location of bed & breakfast places and they pointed me in the direction to St Helier. It was still way too early to be knocking on doors, so I wandered around this lovely town and found a seaman's café which was open. Great. Breakfast.

As it turned out, the locals were wonderfully friendly and probably wondered what on earth I was doing just turning up like this with no forward plans. I found a B&B with a vacant room a few hours later, plonked my stuff down and then fell fast asleep right through to the next morning.

The proprietor of the B&B told me at breakfast time that if you ring a local number in the telephone box, it informs you of any work vacancies; just make sure you take a pen and paper to write them down as it can be a bit quick. Brilliant!

Off I go to the local phone box only to be told there are NO VACANCIES today. Bum! I counted out my money and figured that the cost of the B&B would use it up quite quickly so the next thing to do was find cheaper digs. The boarding house I found was much more to my budget's liking, so I paid one week in advance and tried the telephone job search daily. Unfortunately, still no luck.

The sun was shining though, Hooray!

I met a couple of merchant seamen who decided to take me under their wings. Basically, we went on a pub crawl for the purpose of me asking for work in everyone we called into. Everywhere was fully staffed for the holiday season. I was told that I should have come a month earlier. Oh, the things you find out in hindsight.

I rang Bill to let him know that I've arrived safely and I'm not dead but having no luck with the job situation just yet. He's decided to quit work and come and join me. I've told John and Bob, the two merchant seamen about Bill, but not Bill about John and Bob. Best not. Bill said we could go camping for a while, so I bought a blow-up tent and some other bits and pieces, and Bill brought along other stuff.

I rang Doreen just to say hello and she's now working in Tadsworth Golf Club. Nursing is still on the agenda but not just yet.

Bill arrived and we hired a car for 3 days. We slept in it on the first night because we couldn't find a camp site cheap enough. Unfortunately, you're not allowed to pitch a tent just anywhere.

Next day we head to the information bureau and now armed with a booklet on camp sites we find one in St Brelades which also has hot and cold water, toilets, showers, TV room, shop, playground, 2 cats, Jersey cows, a calf and a donkey.

We pumped up the blow-up tent and the blow-up bed, got cosy and settled. That night it rained and rained and rained. The tent had a sewn in floor and the walls leaked. Not only were we soaked, we also floated. We bailed out the tent, headed for the laundrette and shoved all our wet clothes in the dryer.

Back at the camp site we were told not to have anything touching the tent walls on the inside, that's why it had leaked. You live and learn. AND where was the sunshine? The wind was blowing a gale and the seas were boiling and frothy.

Now two of us were using the telephone job hunting line daily. When the answer was still no vacancies, we'd head off sightseeing.

Jersey has some spectacular scenery with wide sandy beaches, tiny little coves, rocky areas and some fairly steep cliffs. There is a cave called the Devil's Hole which leads to the sea. The Hole is about 100 feet in diameter, and 200 feet deep. The constant smashing of the waves makes it into a kind of blowhole, complete with eerie sucking sounds as the water is pulled down and out into the Channel.

It was originally called *Le Creux de Vis*, or *the Spiral Hollow*, but sometime around 1850 or so the name was changed.

Here is the story of The Devil's Hole:

*It was about 1851 when a ship's carved figurehead was found bobbing up and down inside Le Creux de Vis. The story isn't exactly clear on where it came from—some say it was from a French shipwreck—or how it managed to hit a perfect bullseye and land in the crater. A local craftsman is said to have taken the figure home, fixed it up, added horns, and placed it back along the rim of the basin. From then on, it's been called the Devil's Hole.*

I watched a little dog chasing seagulls out for miles until he just became a dot on the horizon and then charging back in full pelt. I bet he slept well that night.

We went to Mont Orgueil Castle and in each room, there were mannequins made by Madame Tussauds in period costumes with pre-recorded tapes telling of the history. You could spend a whole week in there and still find out that you've missed something.

There is a place called Fantastic Gardens which has been divided into different countries from around the world. It is privately owned and magnificent.

A strawberry farm where you can pick your own and then eat them with fresh Jersey Cream. Yum.

By far the creepiest place we visited was the WW2 German underground hospital, or Ho8. There were story boards telling of the occupation of the Nazi's on the island and the brutality towards some of the workers who built these tunnels.

To brighten the mood after that we headed to St Ouen's beach where the tide was in and crashing spectacularly about 10 feet high onto the sea wall. Smuggler's Inn is an old pub where the locals leave their personal pewter tankards which are hanging from the rafters until they have them filled. You can order Jersey Potatoes which are tiny and served piping hot in small bowls with lashings of Jersey butter. I could live on those. The pub is full of antiquities, sort of felt like an old pirate movie set.

We seemed to have one lousy day after another weather wise and feeling defeated Bill wanted to head for home. Then just in the nick of time I found a job as a Kitchen porter. It meant I had to move into the little rooms that were shared by the other girls that worked in this small hotel. The work was seven days a week with all accommodation and food supplied. Although it was only an eight-hour day, we had to start work at 7.30am and finish at 8.30pm with the chunk in the middle of the day as our free time.

Two of the girls were chambermaids who also became waitresses when needed. Another was the cook and lastly was dish-pan Jenny; me. The hotel could only accommodate about 30 people and the guests all seemed to stay for one week. Not my favourite job and I've never peeled so many potatoes or seen them made into so many dishes. English people seem to need potatoes with every meal. Bloody hell.

The girl I shared the room with also thought nothing of bringing her boyfriend in every night.

I had a special serenade coming form the next bed to mine, charming.

The hotel owner had a beautiful German Shepard dog called Shaun who would love to come walkies with Bill and I in my off-duty time. I discovered that Shaun also loved ice-cream, so we often shared.

Speaking of sharing, Bill met up with a couple of girls who needed somewhere to rest their weary heads and being the gentleman that he was, he offered to let them rest a while in the tent, with him in it. Lucky I'm not the jealous type, probably because I couldn't care less anyway. You only live once.

Time was marching on and the delights of being a kitchen porter was wearing pretty thin. Mum and Dad were going to be in England for my 21st birthday, so Bill and I decided it was time to head back to his family home.

We had a little side trip planned, however. Bill's friend Denis and his wife Georgie were having a caravan holiday in the New Forest for a week, so we joined them pitching our tent in the campgrounds.

The town nearby was called Ringwood and it's so pretty, the forest is home to wild ponies, and we saw plenty of them with their young. We didn't want to cramp Denis and Georgie's style so during the day Bill and I would wander. We'd go about 20 miles a day, I think.

We'd take a bottle of orange juice or some other fluid to keep hydrated on our daily route marches but one particularly hot day we'd drunk it all early. There was a fast-flowing stream, so we refilled our bottles but within no time at all we were vomiting up breakfast. Maybe the animals used this stream as a flush toilet?

A much tastier liquid was the apple cider from the local orchard. We managed to keep that down and buy a few more bottles to keep in reserve.

When we arrived back at Bill's, his family offered to let me stay with them. His little sister had bunk beds and I paid my way by being the cook.

In England the main meal is usually in the middle of the day which they call dinner time. Bill's Dad, Mr. Green, was a shift worker so ate his dinner/breakfast about two o'clock every afternoon. Bob has his at the end of the day, Bill eats whenever his work shift allows him home, Mrs. Green works in the kitchen at Annette's school and they both eat there, so meals were being cooked constantly.

Then I saw an advert for a barmaid back at the Crown, so I rushed in and got the job. The prices had changed but the people hadn't. They knew I wouldn't be around for too long but that didn't bother anyone.

Now I had to get up and have meals cooked by 8.30am and everyone could just reheat when they needed it. Problem solved. One thing for sure though, I will never in my life ever eat slimy tinned peas and instant mashed potato. This family thrived on the ghastly stuff as well as tinned fatty corned beef. Everyone was wary of any form of seasoning and garlic was what you had to keep vampires away...not eat!! If it came in a packet, it was edible, if you created, everyone was dubious.

Bill had gone back to school to become a coach driver. He thought it would only be for three days, but it turned out to be ten days with homework. He was not pleased but I think it was a move in the right direction.

# Chapter 15
# **Mum and Dad Arrive**
## Now I am 21

*Mum, Dad, Me & Bill, in a pub on my 21st birthday*

This was the first holiday my Mum and Dad ever had apart from the voyage to Australia when we migrated thirteen years earlier. Right from the onset Dad wasn't keen on coming back to England just in case Mum wanted to stay. Her sister had just returned after six years in Australia and this was a huge concern to him.

The welcoming party at the airport consisted of Gina and family plus their two friends, Uncle John and Aunty Betty, Bill and I.

Nan and Uncle Peter had decided to go on a holiday just at that exact time. The upside was we could stay in their flat. The downside was Mum was hoping to see Nan. She was her mother and she hadn't seen her in all those years, my Nan is such a strange lady that's for sure.

Bill had borrowed a transit van from work so Dad, Bill and I went together with the luggage, John and Betty took mum and we all met with Gina and family at Nan's flat in Ealing.

Gina had been given the key, but it was the wrong one, so we had to force the window and I scrambled in and opened the door from the inside. Luckily Mr Plod, the policeman, wasn't watching. It would have been a bit of "Ello, 'Ello, Ello, what's going on 'ere then? "Kind of situation.

Once the laughs, hugs and greetings had exhausted themselves and the relatives went home a kindly neighbour gave Mum her spare key and Bill and I left them to sleep the journey off.

The next 5 weeks were a whirlwind of sight-seeing and staying with various relatives. The weather was kind as well. Dad constantly compared and criticised everything, I know he was panicking but it came to a head when Bill's father finally told him that he should just Bugger off back home. I found it quite funny really.

My 21st birthday was memorable that's for sure. I didn't have a specially made cake or even a party. Instead Bill (borrowed) a huge green Double decker bus and the four of us did a London Pub Crawl in style.

It was hilarious as we sped past bus stops with people putting out their hands to hail us down. Haha. We just sailed on by. Mum was drinking Gin and Orange; Bill and Dad were getting into the local brews.

How they all managed to keep standing and as far as Bill was concerned, driving, I'll never know but boy, did they ever pay for it the next day. In fact, Mum never even got that far. She was going green around the gills much earlier on, so Bill took her home, dropped her off to let her suffer alone and in silence and we just kept on rockin'.

When I was twenty-one years and one day old, my parents and boyfriend were "*CACTUS!*".

Mum and Dad thought I'd be going back to Australia with them, but I had other plans. Well, nothing in concrete but I wasn't ready to go home yet. I said that I wanted a job on a ship. Dad said he'd make a deal with me. He would come into London where the shipping offices were and if I didn't get a job, I'd have to go home with them.

Guess what? I came away complete with uniform and starting date which happened to be one day before Mum and Dad were leaving England as a stewardess on a Chandris ship named the Britanis.

*Look out world, here I come.*

*Chapter 16*

# S.S. Britanis

## The Canaries Are Calling

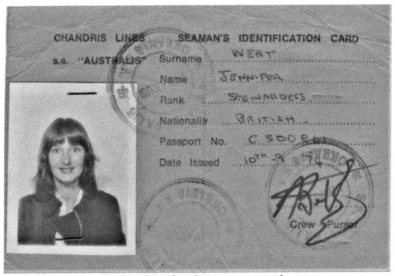

*My Chandris lines crew card*

Photo taken and a Seaman's Identification Card signed and stamped, passport checked, bags packed and maroon skirt, white blouse, new shoes, gold epaulettes, myself and my new uniform were ready. Mum, Dad and Bill drove to Southampton where I boarded the Britanis.

As usual in times of shear panic and fear I completely forget the nitty gritty bits of my memory. I don't remember how I got on board and found my cabin I don't even remember saying goodbye. Just here I was, dressed the same as the other girls in my cabin with a tray shoved in my hand, pointed to a room full of people and said to go and take their drink orders.

At some point we sailed through the Bay of Biscay which is notorious for bringing out the seasickness in even the most seasoned traveller, but I didn't feel a thing. My whole body was so tense there was no room for any other emotions.

There were five of us in a very cramped cabin, but we all worked different hours so were never all in there together except for some stupid hours in the middle of the night.

Vicki seems to have worked here the longest, there is also Annie, another Jenny, Jaye who is an Aussie from Adelaide and I. They are all really nice and very helpful.

The beds were bunks so we had a spare which was lucky because we could plonk our stuff on top of it.

Our cabin had a unique feature in the form of an air vent pipe sporting a dirty great hole. To control the gushes of hurricane like freezing air, towels or blankets were shoved into it. This did hinder our oxygen intake, so a finely balanced amount of stuffing had to be employed.

One of the girls and I'm not saying which one was obviously a bit of a sex maniac. The posters of full-frontal nude males plastered all over the cabin walls was enough to turn you off your sausages and potatoes, or in my case being a vegetarian, bananas and coconuts.

Another Cat Stevens song came to mind, *You can't keep it in'*. Oh well, we didn't have a port hole, so some scenery was needed I suppose.

My bunk didn't have any pillows, so I asked the chief steward, Triphon, who's actually my boss where to get them. He took me up to his cabin and gave me his; *hmm.*

My working hours were from twelve noon until 4pm, then again from 7.30pm until 2am. The cabin has no port holes (or air when pipe is jammed with bed clothes!) so I had to rely on my little travel clock. I never saw breakfast and quite often missed lunch, but I managed dinner before starting my second shift. Triphon usually turned up with some food at 2am but by then I wasn't really that hungry, just tired.

Lisbon was our first port of call and a waiter called Theo took Jenny and I ashore with him. We were all having a great time even though Theo's English wasn't too good, and my Greek was non-existent but just before we boarded the ship he asked if I would like to go to Greece with him in October and marry him. **WHAT!!**

I thought he'd got his words mixed up but when I saw him again, he asked me once more. He said we'd get our wedding rings in Las Palmas and his father has a house and wants him to have a nice girl, and that was me. **YIKES!**

Now all I had to do was ask my parents. *Whew,* I could see a way out. I told him my parents would probably say no and he cried. SHIT! He knew my working hours, so I had to learn the sacred art of dodging and hiding very quickly. This was easy enough to do because I kept getting lost on the ship anyway.

I did manage to lose him but then there was the chief steward who was 35 years old, and two other waiters, one was 25 years old and the other 22 all asking the same question. Just to make matters even more confusing I had passengers wanting my home address as well. Great for the ego but I was doing more 'Soft Shoe Shuffling' than Fred Astaire. I even bought a wig and wore that in my off-duty hours, so they didn't think I was me. Seemed to work anyway.

After Lisbon we sailed into Madeira where the wine was cheap and pretty rough. They store it in great barrels and then roll these barrels down a long, straight, steep alley; you wouldn't want to get in the way.

I went for a local bus ride up to the top of the town and then back again, it was steeper and more terrifying than Acapulco, but the locals didn't seem to be fazed at all. Tenerife was another beautiful island in Grand Canaria with warm sunshine and smiling people. I took myself off on a horse and buggy ride. The buggy was all decorated with brightly coloured tassels with a fringe on top.

Down to Dakar; this was dusty and bustling and very African. I'd never seen anything like it before. The sounds and smells were quite engulfing. I bought a large Kora which is a stringed instrument with a large bowl body a wooden neck and strings. God knows why because I can't play any musical instrument and where the hell would I keep it anyway. I think the country got to me.

I worked the evening shift in the Ballroom when we docked in Las Palmas and I don't think there was one passenger still on board. The ship was there all day and we weren't due to sail until about 3am. Jaye was working in one of the other lounges and as bored as I was.

Most of the crew were at The Piano Bar where I'd been until duty called. It was so much fun and felt very sophisticated. The chief steward came by to make sure I'd cleaned all the ashtrays and had everything looking spick and span, in other words he was bored as well. I asked if Jaye and I could go ashore again as there was nothing to do. He said we'd have to ask the Staff Captain.

When the Staff Captain cruised by and I asked, well, not really, I begged him to let us go ashore. He wanted to know why, and I said there was nothing to do here and I was bored. A wicked glint came in his eyes and he simply gave me his cabin key, he assured me that I wouldn't be bored. He also said to Jaye that we could come together. We did go together as it happened, only not to his cabin but back to the piano bar with the fun crowd. We got back on board just before sailing and continued the party in the band's cabins.

Then I heard that the Master at Arms was searching for me. O Oh. The Staff Captain's key. I still had it. Whoops! I gave the key to one of the guys in the band and like the coward that I am, I hid. Old Staff Captain wasn't a *Happy Chappy*. As it turned out he realised that neither Jaye nor I were going to turn up so he turned his attention to a glamorous unsuspecting (or maybe suspecting) passenger but couldn't get into his cabin. I was later to pay for my mistake.

Casablanca was exciting. Jaye and I went together and felt very brave. Shopping in the Kasbah without a man to chaperone us. We bought beautiful kaftans with lace and applique. I loved the palm trees all dripping with dates and the old intricately decorated buildings.

Vigo in Spain was beginning to get chilly and it felt a bit too normal after the other ports we'd visited. It also seems that when the weather is cold, so are the people.

My misdemeanour with the staff captain was catching up with me now. He told Jaye and I that our work would be terminated in Southampton and we would have to leave. Not happy about that at all I had a word in the ear of other crew members, and some were more influential. Stephanos was an engineer and obviously quite high ranking. Someone worth knowing as it turned out. Both Jaye and I got to stay aboard until the end of these two cruises.

Back in Southampton the first cruise passengers disembarked and the second lot boarded. By this time, I was an old hand and I'd also got my sleeping patterns sorted so didn't look like something the cat dragged in when we had early morning lifeboat drills. Mind you I always dreaded them because the captain would quiz the crew and as I hadn't bothered to read never mind memorise my Little White Book, I had no idea what I was supposed to do in case of an emergency. I just knew that crew stood nearer to the lifeboats than the passengers did. Suits me.

We called into Rotterdam, then a group of us took a taxi into Amsterdam. Bloody cold and rainy but I somehow love this place. Maybe it's because everyone can speak English and the buildings are so pretty and unique. The cakes and hot chocolate are always worth a tasting as well.

I did this trip twice before disembarking in Southampton. The Britanis was going into Dry Dock for maintenance. The stewards and stewardesses were going home. The multiple nationalities that made up the remaining crew either found work on other ships or took this opportunity to have a well-earned break. Many hadn't been home for months.

## Chapter 17

# The Unsuspecting Stowaway

## Nowhere to Hide

After the first cruise Bill was at the docks to meet me. He'd been in a bit of a scuffle with a bus and came off worse. Stephanos took one look at him and didn't want me to go ashore. What could I do? Old lover or new lover? Well I did go ashore and found out that there was no real need to worry.

The end of the second cruise meant that most of the crew went home. Apparently, the ship had hit an iceberg up near Russia or the North Cape. These were the cruises before I joined and had been temporarily patched up. Glad I didn't know that before I'd joined the crew. I had seen Titanic!

The Greeks to Greece, the Brits to Britain and me, well, nowhere!! Steve who was the lifeguard on the ship lived with two other guys in Hampstead and there was a spare bed if I wanted it. It belonged to one of the guys he only sees about two weeks every six months or so. Great. We got a lift with Fiona, another stewardess who lives in Bromley and stayed for a cuppa with her mum, then by train to Steve's place. Everything was going to plan.

Until Timmy. Yes, you've guessed it, the long-lost flatmate along with Brian, the other flatmate turned up. Steve didn't say anything so I thought I'd just play it by ear and see what would happen. Well, Steve and I went out for dinner and then to a pub and met a crowd of his mates. Back to Steve's and more people had arrived. Eventually I fell asleep on the floor. (Explanation needed here. I hadn't slept for 2 days because of all the farewell parties on board).

The next day, Mike one of Steve's friends asked me out for dinner. He was over 6-foot-tall, 29 years old and a producer for the BBC. I described him because I thought all BBC producers would have been old blokes of about 50 or 60. Don't know why, just did.

Anyway, good old Steve sorted my sleeping arrangements out for me. He slept at his girlfriend's and I slept in his bed. He knew it was only for a short stay because Stephanos had asked me to go to Rotterdam as another engineer's girlfriend was also coming and we would share an apartment together until the ship was fixed and cruises started again, this time for the Caribbean.

I booked my bus fare and Steve came with me to Victoria Station and we said our goodbyes. I slipped him five pounds in a thank you letter.

The bus took about 3 hours to get to Dover and drove straight onto the ferry. Upstairs on the ferry I found a comfy chair and settled down with a book, sandwich and a cup of coffee. A man asked if I'd mind his bag and a seat whilst he went and got himself a cuppa, we ended up keeping each other company for the journey. He was a travelling salesman I think and bunging it on a bit with a *Big Man* attitude. I tried to outshine him by telling him that I'm a stewardess on a cruise ship and have just finished the Canary Island cruises.

Eventually we got our levels sorted out and bragging rights done the conversation was much more relaxed.

Just before we got off the ferry though, he said if I see a blue Jag, it'll be him. BUM! Got me. I wish I'd said, well if you see a big white Mercedes, it'll be me. Well that was the make of the bus anyway.

It took another 4 hours to get to Rotterdam and then a taxi to the Dry Docks where I was to meet Stephanos.

There seemed to be millions of blokes working at the docks and they all whistled and carried on when I walked along searching for the ship. Embarrassed and uncomfortable.

I haven't mentioned this before, but I have a shocking and humiliating habit of blushing. It has plagued me all my life and at this very time it showed itself in the best technicolour possible.

It was 8.30am and I'd been travelling since 8 o'clock the night before. You'd think I'd be used to no sleep by now, but I was buggered. Stephanos took me to his cabin and I fell asleep until midday. George, the other engineer who was going to be sharing an apartment with us and his girlfriend told us that he's been transferred to the Ellinis, another Chandris ship.

I had a funny feeling this was a set up and I'm now officially a stow-away on a dry-docked ship. Still didn't have to pay for rent or food but it did mean that long embarrassing walk past all the workmen whenever I snuck off or on the ship. Also, I wasn't actually allowed to be there.

This is how we solved the problem.

Every morning a group of Stephanos's friends would crowd around me and we'd all walk in a huddle to the gate then I was free for the day. I quickly learnt how to buy bus and train tickets and made myself scarce as well as useful for the guys who wanted shopping or letters posted etc.

One of the guys asked me to write a letter to his girlfriend in New York and tell her when we would be there next time. No problem, I did that for him and then read out what I wrote. With that he opened his wallet and showed me photos of about ten different girls and asked if I'd write to them as well.

Yep, a typical sailor.

At night we would gather at the gates and do the reverse. Sometimes we'd all just head back into town by taxi and go to the movies or a restaurant or nightclub.

One night we saw a movie called **It's Alive"** and it was a horror. I fell off my seat when I jumped in fright and the seat folded up behind me. A millisecond later all 8 Greeks did the same thing. My scream made them all jump. All their seats instantly folded and all their bums hit the floor in unison. The audience seated behind found it very amusing.

Stowing away on a ship in dry dock had its advantages, like free rent, a bed and food but it also had many disadvantages, like no hot water and I wasn't even supposed to be there. I was secreted away in Stephanos's cabin. He rigged up a metal oil heater and with a large metal bucket which I filled with water and left on all night.

Next morning, I managed to have a warm water wash taking the bucket into the shower cubicle then hand wash and hang out my clothes in there as well. Problem was, I had to share the shower space with the other engineer in the adjoining cabin and he had an uncanny knack of barging in at the most inappropriate times.

We did have a bit of fun whilst I'd been stranded there though. The guys sometimes got parcels of food from home and then they choose a cabin to cook their feast up in. They use my oil heater as the cooker.

Some of the stuff looks revolting, dried octopus, unripened walnuts mixed with marmalade and yoghurt, orange flower petals dripping in syrup (that was quite nice but sooooo sweet).

One day coming back from Rotterdam the ship had disappeared. Panic! I went searching and found this time it was really in dry dock. Last time it was still floating in shallow water, now it was about half a mile further away and totally out of the water.

The ship is absolutely huge. Also, I now have to do the walk of shame alone as the guys don't want to keep coming out all that way to shield me, especially as it was so bloody cold in November.

The only way I could re-join the ship as crew was to sign on in England. That meant making my way back to London's Chandris office. It was time to march that long harassing, wolf whistling, and excruciatingly embarrassing walk for one last time before I headed back to England.

*Chapter 18*

# **Welcome Back**

## Well, sort of

*Me, Vicky (front) and Denise
Denise and I were stewardesses
and Vicky was a cashier on the S.S. Britanis.*

Guess who met me at the airport. Yep it was good old Bill, we're just mates now. He realised that there was no way I wanted to settle down and become a busman's bride but still some fun was on the agenda before heading back to the high seas. With old Morris, the car given to him as a thank you by my parents when they came for a holiday, we decided that a quick trip from top to bottom of Wales like we'd done once before but this time as two old mates. We went halves with the petrol, slept in the car and only stopped at cafes for a pee a bite to eat and a cup of coffee. It was a brilliant couple of days.

A quick visit to see John and Betty, sorted out clothes and left a ton of stuff with them to look after, lots of goodbyes and laughter and off to Gatwick airport for my flight to Amsterdam to re-join my work, accommodation and everything else for the next 6 months on the Britanis.

Bill and I waved until we disappeared from each other's sight. He was a terrific guy and quite genuine, but we were ships that passed in the night, somehow. I've still got the beautiful gold watch he gave me for my 21st birthday though and the memories. Hope he hasn't totally forgotten me after all these years.

I was back in the same cabin complete with gaping hole in the air vent hanging perilously close to the luckless person who gets the short straw for that particular top bunk. Funny how nobody thought it worthwhile fixing. This time there are six of us, so someone has to have it. Three old girls two newbies and me.

We were off to the warmth of the Caribbean and as an added bonus, no passengers until we got there. The downside.... there is ALWAYS a downside. We had to wash, polish and scrub the old tub until it gleamed. Working from eight o'clock in the morning until the evening when scrubbing brushes down and music in the disco cranked up, it was party time.

The ship was scheduled to do two, one-week cruises alternating between some of the ports. Embarkation was always San Juan, Puerto Rico every Monday. La Guaira in Venezuela every Friday and Curacao every Saturday. Sunday was our day at sea. The other ports were

Guadeloupe or St Thomas on Tuesdays, Barbados or Martinique Wednesdays and St Vincent, every second Thursday with a once off visit to St Croix, Dominican Republic, Jamaica, Tobago and a couple of times to Grenada and Santa Domingo. My greatest fear was to be in a once only port and I had to work without the time for exploration. It can happen.

My first timetable was from 2pm until 6pm then 9pm until 3am in the Smoke Bar. So, yet again, breakfast was a mystery of life.

San Juan, Monday. On came the passengers and off went our party nights in the disco. It was fun while it lasted and I got to meet a tall, dark and handsome Welsh man called David, which was a lucky find because Stephanos's Greek girlfriend had joined the crew, so I was pushed sideways. He was quite comfortable to accommodate both of us, with only me knowing about her and not the other way around, but I declined his over amorous offer and went in search of new pastures, which I soon found in the form of the fore mentioned Welsh Croupier.

Another tall dark guy keeps turning up and wanting all my attention but only ever asks for peanuts or matches and calls me Juanita. Lifeboat drill he needed my help with his jacket which he'd purposely tied in a million knots and I had to untie them all. Smooth or what? Still he'd be off in a few days so I could put up with it. Well that would have been the case if he was a passenger and not in the band which I found out later. Oh well, back to the old Soft Shoe Shuffle again.

St Croix was our next port of call. It's one of the British Virgin Islands but it nearly stuffed up our cruises. Someone rammed the ship into the pier. God we'd only been here two days!! And all that work fixing up the old barge in Rotterdam gone to waste. But as it turned out after countless hours and a team of scuba divers, they managed to patch her up again and send us on our way. I hoped the sticky tape lasts the distance.

Once I got into the rhythm of the strange working hours and the persistent attempts of just about all the males on the ship, mainly crew but also the occasional pesky passenger wanting to get to know the nether regions of my torso and I ceased being constantly tried. I enjoyed both my work and all the excitement these beautiful islands had to offer.

Our Chief Steward, although a grumpy bastard at times also let all of us girls sort out the going ashore times. Our work rosters seem to change fairly frequently as well as the bars that we worked in but after a few months both the barmen and stewardesses had their **favourites and we managed** to work with the ones we liked best.

Gerda, Ginger, Anna, Annie, Angela and I were roomies.

Gerda and Ginger were both from the Netherlands, so Curacao was a real favourite for them because of the Dutch connection. Angela was a gentle, fun loving English lady. She was our age but much more sophisticated than us, but we soon educated her in the ways of the wild. Anna was Australian but with Dutch heritage, Annie was Australian and as stubborn as a mule, in fact quite the opposite to Angela and I must admit to being extremely hard to get along with. Of course, I was perfect in every way.

Ginger by name and ginger by colour. I've never met anyone who sunbathes in the extreme way that she did. I got horribly sunburnt once and my face glowed bright red. The guys in the band would call out "HOW" when I walked past because I looked like a Red Indian, but Ginger looked like that all the time.

Her hair was hennaed, and she managed to adjust her bikini top to only keep her nipples from burning. Instead of having round areola, hers were perfectly square. Just thought you'd like to know that. Her English was also atrocious which is very uncommon for anyone from Holland. She really was a dumb blonde in disguise, and I thought she was fabulous. Once when she was hennaing her hair, she fell asleep and it kept on cooking. It was the most fluorescent fire engine red that you've ever seen. Needless to say, she got noticed.

Gerda was one tough cookie, but she had a soft side and great fun if she was on your side I'll tell you a bit more about her later. We boarded the ship in Amsterdam early December 1975 and the cruises finished back in Amsterdam in May 1976 therefore we had Christmas, New Year, Easter and Greek Easter plus many, many Name days which are all causes for celebration.

We had love affairs, broken hearts, grumbles, mumbles and side-splitting laughter all mixed in with stupid hours, sunburn, tiredness, drunkenness and you only get time off if you are nearly dead. What's not to love about cruising? The tips were pretty good because the Americans and Canadians were used to that sort of thing and it didn't take us long to get used to that sort of thing either. In fact, we were very put out if at least a quarter of a dollar didn't hit the tray with every serve of drinks.

In my first three days I made $45 in tips and $10 of that got stolen from my tray so I bought a pouch purse which I wore around my waist to keep the notes in. The passengers could be a whole lot of fun especially if you were cheeky back to them. One guy wanted three whiskies and three kisses. I kissed him on top of his head and got $5 tip for my trouble.

Yannis was a steward but thought he'd boss me around. He kept saying, Ashtrays, Ashtrays!" I asked him what he thought I was doing. I think he thought I spent most of my time mucking around and flirting with passengers, which was possibly true, but I can also do my work at the same time. I nearly told him to go jump overboard, which would have been messy as we were in port at the time. Maybe a punch on his nose would have fixed the problem.

Christmas Eve on the ship really didn't feel all that festive. We'd pinched a plastic bush from the Marine Bar and decorated it up like a Christmas tree for our cabin.

Bought each other gifts and placed them underneath. Angela made us Christmas stockings and crackers which she'd stashed miniature bottles of spirits into. What a great idea. We bought booze in St Thomas and when I finished work at 3am Christmas morning everyone was woken up.

Gerda & I went and pinched lemonade, coke, ice and glasses from the bar. My Fijian cassette player was cranked up and the party began. Apart from the six of us we also had three stewards, the casino guys, and six passengers all crammed in. We danced, drank and sung until we could stand no more. A couple of the girls blurringly dragged themselves off to work at 10.30am and the rest of us cleaned up the carnage.

We docked in Martinique on Christmas day, but we were leaving at

12.30pm so no time to go anywhere. Instead, David and I sat nursing our hangovers on the docks with the steel drum band bashing away and small native children amusing the passengers with their diving skills when coins were thrown into the water for them.

We had a crew Christmas party on Boxing day evening but that wasn't as much fun as ours, so I headed for bed.

31st December 1975 and we were in Barbados. I didn't get up early enough to go ashore as I had to start work at 2pm. The passengers were going to be given free champagne at midnight, so we all had to polish champagne glasses. I think about 300 each would have been a fair estimate as well as the normal serving and cleaning bloody ashtrays, still the tips were brilliant. I made $118 and told Yannis to "PISS OFF, what a lady I was.

January meant another reshuffle of hours and bars. Now I was in the Ballroom every evening and whichever bar needed a stewardess in the daytime. We girls covered for each other making sure everyone got a chance to go ashore. A skeleton crew on during the day was all that was needed.

Occasionally you got a killer shift which was starting early straight after a 4am finish the previous night. Then if Lifeboat drill was thrown into the mix, which happened far too often, I'd be walking around in a dream like daze.

Ginger had got a boyfriend in Curacao and I went with them to a beach near the Hilton hotel. He was a deep-sea diver photographer and his friends were all divers. They would free dive for Black Coral and then polish it up, mount it onto silver and make jewellery.

They lived a very dangerous life because apart from having no scuba gear and the depths they dived down to get the coral, they also had to be aware of sharks.

We had a really fun day and even though I thought I had a suntan, everyone called me Snow White. Well they were all dark skinned and Ginger was living up to her name, so fair enough I suppose. When they gave us a lift back to the ship one of the divers gave me a Black Coral necklace.

I had a curious week in late January.

A passenger I served a drink to hadn't changed his money to US dollars so I said he could pay me later. It was only 80 cents, so it didn't break the bank. Well later he found me in the Ballroom and asked me to serve him his drinks all night. At the end his drink total came to $5.80 and he gave me $20 and said keep the change.

Next day he gave me a bottle of French perfume and again only wanted me to serve him. This turned out a real winner for me because I always got a large tip at the end of the night.

His home was in Curacao, that's why he didn't have US Dollars when he first boarded and offered to show me around the island. That can always be a bit dodgy so I could always blame odd working hours to get out of sticky situations like that without any feelings getting hurt. He also asked how many girls I shared a cabin with, so I told him, and he bought them all boxes of chocolates so they wouldn't get jealous of me. His name was Harold.

The next intake of passengers in San Juan was a group of about 400 who belonged to some convention called METRO. They bought their own alcohol and Yannis had to set up a bar just for them. This turned out to be a bit of a nightmare. I had to serve them with drinks from their bar and not charge them and the other passengers from the normal bar. Back and forth all week and if they didn't have their METRO badge on I'd get it wrong and it would cost me as I had to buy the drinks out of my own money and whatever tips I got were mine to keep.

Tips were my main source of income because wages weren't given to us until the cruise was over. I don't know how the cashier's managed as they hardly ever got tips. So, you can imagine that cursed things like cocktail parties put a hole in the night's takings.

I always seemed to get the job of serving the Captain's table and the tray was extremely heavy. Yannis said it was good for building my muscles, I said it was perfect because I could then give him a good punch on the nose. I was told it was an honour, serving the Staff Captain or Captain and their guests. I considered it a real bummer.

One night the Staff Captain was entertaining the dancers and asked me to get him Benson & Hedges, I said just one or the packet. He gave me a look and said that I knew what he meant. So I got a packet of the cigarettes, opened it, gave him one and kept the rest. He pulled my hair and laughed then invited me to join them, I couldn't of course because I was working but he said I was the best stewardess because I was always so happy and smiling.

What he really meant was cheeky, flirty and rude.

Another non tipping time is buffet preparation. We all have to take in turns doing that mind-numbing job which consists of rolling a knife, fork and spoon in a serviette and stack them onto a tray. I would work in the Ballroom from 6.30pm until 11pm then buffet duty until 1am and then back to the Ballroom until 3am.

I did have fun with passengers though. Not just the men, I was also cheeky to their wives and girlfriends. It paid off because apart from the tips I also received the occasional silly gift like a T-shirts that said "Pure...Not by chance but by law...Puerto Rican Rum." Or "I'm a Virgin" from St Thomas, not sure I'd wear them around much. Sometimes even a pretty necklace or a souvenir of some sort. One guy gave me a small plastic box and in it was a pair of bright yellow knickers. All evening long I heard the call of "Show us your knickers" much to the amusement of the punters.

Most of the shore time was taken with friends but sometimes I'd share a taxi tour with passengers. One of those times was in Guadeloupe. The town wasn't all that exiting so a Canadian couple, Yannis (yes, the same Yannis I wanted to punch in the nose) and I headed into the country side. There were natives carrying huge bundles piled high on their heads, a river with round rocks where they would do their washing and all around the sweet smell of cooked sugar. That was because of the sugar cane that grew and was milled for the rum factory. We saw banana plantations, pineapples growing like weeds and cocoa trees. The taxi driver stopped and cracked open a cocoa pod and the smell of chocolate was delicious. There were also coconut trees and coffee plants, so different to the town's people way of life.

One day in Grenada eight of us girls hired a yacht which two men sailed. They took us to a little cove and threw a rope over so we could jump into the water and use the rope to pull ourselves back on board. We snorkelled around and saw some beautiful fish in this very deep inlet. The men told us that back in the 1700's the entire French fleet was hiding in this cove but were found and captured by the British.

We did scuttle back on board fairly quickly though when he told us the lone one-legged black fisherman in the little dingy close to us had lost his leg fighting off a shark.

The Britanis was told that we would be meeting up with the Australis, but the dates constantly changed. A lot of the Greek crew had family on board the other ship. It could be brothers or cousins and they hadn't seen each other in months. Sometimes we were told it would be Puerto Rico other times Curacao.

Well it finally happened. We met up finally in February and the excitement was electric even for the crew who hadn't got anyone or even seen the Australis before. I couldn't wait to get on board and see if Nick was still working there. My Mum had said that they'd received a Christmas card from him. How nice was that?

Well, all the Australis passengers were crowding out the gangplank and I was too impatient to wait so climbed in through the doorway that lead to the kitchens. It was a bit tricky, but the guys caught me as I leapt in as there was no gangplank or even a step there.

I saw Nick and he found it funny that I was now crew and not a passenger anymore. He said once they reach England the ship will head to Greece and he plans on getting off and catching up with his family. Maybe we'll meet up again when this cruise ends in May.

The poor old Australis did look like it needed a holiday, well a damn good wash and paint anyway. I didn't realise that a ship can actually look tired.

La Guaira is the port of Venezuela that we called into every Friday. It has quite magnificent scenery with forested mountains that loom over the port. Caracas is the capital city and there are two ways to get to it. One is by car, or in our case taxi. The road is big and wide but all along the sides are crowded shanty towns. Thousands of people live there and are obviously very poor. There is a huge divide between rich and poor here. The cars are immaculate, the petrol is so cheap. Phillips is one of the main companies and as we drove along this well-maintained road up and over the mountain and coming into the city you could see the evidence of extreme wealth.

The other way to get to Caracas is much more fun. You ascend the mountain by Teleférico de Caracas, a cable car that slowly climbs up 7000 feet into the clouds then descends down and the magical landscape of the huge city emerges.

I did this trip many times but once I was alone and decided just to explore locally. I hired a taxi and my driver couldn't speak English and I can't speak Spanish, so we sign language the whole time. He took me to local bars and all over the place. When it was time to head back to the ship, he wouldn't take any money, I gave him $10 anyway. That was probably too much, but I'd had a great time. Only problem from then on was, he always met the ship and kept calling for me.

18 carat gold is also inexpensive here and I couldn't resist buying a snake link chain to wear around my waist.

For two of the cruises we had the reigning Miss World. She was so beautiful and everywhere in Caracas her photos or posters abound. She came aboard with her equally beautiful sister who was a local movie star. I don't think any eyes of any males, even the gay ones, left their sight. But there was a sad tale about Miss World. She had an incurable bone disease and if she didn't inject herself daily, she was as ridged as a stone. She lived for one more year and her sister was her carer. So sad, but you never have known because they always had the most radiant smiles.

Harold from Curacao turned up at the ship and came to see me. He was a passenger one or two cruises earlier and presented me with a bracelet of 14 carat gold. I was stunned and said I couldn't possibly accept it, but he insisted. It cost him 286 Gilders which was about $143 US. I only knew the price because he also gave me the guarantee. Then he started sending me telegrams wanting to meet up and has even offered to pay for a holiday in Curacao.

I met an American guy named Les on the docks one day in San Juan whilst killing time before my shift started. He works in the radio room of an ocean-going, tug and he's from New York so I told him we'd be going there on our way back to Europe when these cruises finish. Valentine's Day came and so did a giant card and an invitation to stay with him in America when the ship gets to New York.

I felt like I was becoming a real sailor with a man in every port!!

Passengers on these cruises are a real mixed bunch. Mainly they are middle aged, plain, fun loving couples escaping the chill of the Canadian or American winter; however, we do get some interesting ones as well.

One time, Gerda turned up with a stray girl. She found her crying in the hallway because the boy she'd been going out with for the last two years and came on this cruise with was a real prick, so she'd left him. Not knowing what to do, Gerda offered a bunk in our room. We always had at least one bunk spare as we all had boyfriends by now and quite often didn't come home at night. Anyway, the girl stayed and came ashore with us as well. The barmen felt sorry for her and she never paid for a drink for the whole cruise.

A much more interesting group were the whores. Four of them in fact. Miss Vicki was at least seven-foot-tall, and we were told she'd had *The Operation*, Francine was a Madame of a House of Pleasure, Bobby, who looked the straightest and DD who sported many scratches on her neck.

DD said she got them when she bought someone back to the cabin and there was a jealousy fight. Many a male crew member looked after these four beauties with undivided attention. I think their fare was well and truly covered even with added interest. How good is that? A profitable holiday.

A place the crew could sunbathe without passengers was the boat deck. A bit squishy with all sorts of ship stuff stored in metal boxes and ropes and other bits and pieces all over the place but you could find a sheltered sunny spot if you got there early enough.

I decided to climb the Crow's Nest, great view, also you could hang over the Britanis sign from the boat deck, just had to keep an eye out for any spoil sport Master at Arms or other officers who deemed this type of behaviour dangerous. Still, got my photos to prove that I did it, and so did David.

Being out in the open with all the reflections from the sea and of course the wind, it was too easy to get sun burnt. We weren't immune to it even after the full six months and I could never stay too long.

Once in Barbados I was able to get a whole afternoon off and didn't have to start work until the evening. I went with the casino mob and a dancer and this time to a different beach called Sandy Lane with towels, bathers and a picnic.

There we met up with some French guys, one had a beautiful German Shepard dog and we bought our drinks from the nearby bar. We were all having a great time but unfortunately the sun was a bit too strong and by the time I got back to work the dreaded sun stroke had hit me. As I mentioned before, you only stop work minutes before you drop dead and I felt just like that.

The good old Aussie nurses looked after me and my grumpy boss was given a forged doctor's note so I could take the night off to recover.

This only happened twice in the whole six months of working seven days a week. The other time I got a fine, but I managed to get that overturned. I worked it out that my pay was in British money the grand total of 2.62 British Pounds a day and I didn't collect that until I got back to England. I know I had my meals and board but when I worked up to sometimes 16 hours a day, I think the occasional sick day is allowed.

Working in the Ballroom meant I got to see the shows, sometimes twice a night but strangely they were never boring or monotonous.

Jimmy the compare was brilliant the way he enticed so-called mild-mannered people, mainly blokes from the audience up on stage and got them to do the most humiliating things.

I would quite often work in cahoots with him and stand behind unsuspecting passengers pointing out the ones who were cheeky to me or big, fat, hairy guys and he would say they were all ex Moulin Rouge dancers and had the operation.

After making complete fools of themselves they would always say they would kill me but in reality, I usually got more tips. The dancers had so many dance routines that I never bored of seeing them either. The bands were great and when it was a themed night, they always played the right type of music.

Between shows meant a mad clean up and that was always fraught with being hassled by Yannis. One time the room was still full of passengers walking too slowly, so I did a short cut back to the bar, tray stacked high with empty glasses, tripped over a table, a passenger tried to save me but came down for the ride with glasses splattering everywhere.

The next day just happened to be yet another bloody cocktail party and with those a bit of added danger, we have to wear white cotton gloves. This makes holding onto an over laden tray feel like gripping melted butter.

I did it again, this time the ship was *Rocking and Rolling,* and I flew over some chairs. The crowd cheered!

If that wasn't bad enough, later that same night, I split beer all over the table missing the glass completely as the ship lurched, another time without spilling a drop this time I landed on some poor guys lap.

Funny enough, everyone laughed and cheered every time I had a mishap. Anyone would think I was the entertainment. I certainly was the floor show, that's for sure.

Harold from Curacao came back for another cruise and with that loads more gifts and tips. David and Yannis were watching me like hawks. I'm sure they thought I was getting off with this guy, but I didn't.

The girls in my cabin thought it was hysterically funny. They said, if he wants to shower you with gifts, just take them and if he wants to give them anything, they'll be happy about that as well. Then I found out the real reason for all these gifts and attention.

One of the dining room waiters came up to me and asked if I knew Harold, I said I did, and he gave me loads of presents. The waiter told me that he is actually married but prefers men, so he's been to bed with him and an entertainment officer as well. He was just using me as a front. That's why he never put the hard word on me, now all I had to do was convince David and Yannis. Lucky me.

March 14th is Greek name day for Benedictus and Efrassios. *Party Time!!* Yet another one down in the dining room when all passengers should be tucked up in their beds.

I wonder if passengers know that their place of fine dining is a place of debauchery most evenings. There are so many Greek name days.

One evening though a drunken female passenger found out and decided to colour the evening with a bit of personal strip tease. I left pretty soon after that, I wonder how she got on.

Here's a joke for you.

*A German man went up to an English Lady and said "Ve vill go out if you vish" So they went to the movies and had a good time.*

*"Ve vill go to a restaurant if you vish" So a night of fine dining was had.*

*"Ve vill go to your place now if you vish" Back at her place they had coffee and a bit of how's your father.*

*Next morning he says to her "In 9 months' time you vill have a baby and you can call him Hans if you vish" She said "in 9 weeks' time, you will have a little rash, you can call it measles if you vish."*

Speaking of such things; we always looked out for the Staff Captain's next conquest. It was a fun thing we girls used to entertain ourselves doing as we hung over the railing watching new passengers embark.

Most of the time we got it right as well. Some of the time, we had chosen the correct girl, but she wouldn't have anything to do with him. That's when it got a bit tricky for me. I think he figured I was a good stand in.

Once when I was working in the bar closest to his cabin, he rang down to the barman and I was told to take a tray with two drinks on it up to his cabin. Up I went, knocked on the door and told to enter.

There he was in all his glory. **YIKES**!

I went to bolt out the room, but he quickly shoved a chair in front of the door.

Hmm, was this his idea of foreplay?

A bit of wrestling and me still fully clothed...just... and him in a slightly precarious position, I managed to escape. Readjusting my twisted skirt, tucked back in my shirt, hand brushed my hair, I walked back into the bar and gave the barman a right mouthful.

We always knew when the Staff Captain had a bout of the 'Measles" because he drank plain orange juice for about a week. Alcohol and antibiotics don't mix apparently.

There were more Aussies and Kiwi's working for Chandris than you would have imagined. For me and I'm sure for the others as well it was a great way to see the world in relative safety and a whole lot of fun.

A group of us got together and Paul the photographer took our photo all holding cans of Fosters. Just then the Captain came down and told us off. He thought we were advertising but even though Paul tried to explain that we were just having a bit of fun, I don't think he actually believed it. Oh well, Paul gave us each a photo for free anyway.

25th March Greek National Day and Angelo the barman's name day. Everyone was in a good mood, even grumpy Yannis and barmen who you'd think a smile would crack their faces are sporting more than a mere smirk.

One of the stewards whose name is also Yannis, but I'll call him John, dressed in traditional Greek costume which consisted of a white puffy shirt, white pleated skirt (a mini at that) white tights, Blue bolero jacket and pom-pommed shoes. Very becoming. He could really dance, and it was very exciting. The band played all the Greek music, the Captain and Staff Captain (don't know who was driving tonight) danced the Kalimatinos and plates were smashed all over the floor. Mad buggers.

April came and here we go again, polishing everything that stands still. This time it was for the Health Inspectors. They came aboard quite often and the most complained about item was the amount of chlorine in the water. I must admit, it did taste like a swimming pool but most passengers wouldn't even know it, who drank water anyway when the alcohol was so cheap?

We had actors and photographers on board hamming it up and getting special treatment. They were here to promote the next lot of cruises and also for the catalogues. Everyone looked very polished and elegant, not quite reality.

I started buying clothes that were a bit warmer. Only 3 more complete cruises to go before we headed to New York. I bought a bright red boiler suit with an American flag on the front and a Shell sign on the back. One of the dancers put her sunglasses on because she said it was so bright, Yannis said I looked like either an astronaut or a garage attendant. Oh well, my white trouser suit was more subtle I suppose.

All the girls got moved around again and even three of the dining room girls are up in the bars now. The reason for this was an influx of about 400 Venezuelans. Obviously, the staff who'd done this before knew about them. We didn't! They were rude and bloody hard work. Constantly demanding, ice, peanuts and our attention. No tips and no manners. Glad they were only there for a week.

Speaking of rude, I had another little angle when I was working in the Marine bar. He asked if he could just pay for his drinks at the end of the night. I said OK but as I have to pay for the drinks myself and I only have a $10 float, it could be difficult.

With that he hailed me with sarcasm and then gave me $100. A bit of a prick I thought but I took his $100 and kept it separate. He bought everyone drinks and got smashed in the process and at the end of the night I gave him his $71 change back and the bastard didn't tip me.

That meant I didn't get tips from everyone he bought drinks for as well. Learnt a lesson, never do that again. Next day, he was back with an almighty hangover and a cloud of guilt. He did tip me, so I forgave him and made sure the music in the bar was loud and tinny.

That's called revenge!

The Flu, Oh My God. It has slugged so many of the crew. Whether

107

it came aboard with a passenger or it was caught from shore, we don't know but watching even the strongest go down like a ton of sweaty, hot bricks takes your breath away. I think it was called Swine Flu and it started in New Jersey apparently.

Those of us who didn't get it had to work extra shifts to cover for the rest. I worked from 9.30 in the morning until 12.30 next morning with just quick breaks to grab something to eat.

It was exhausting but we couldn't show it as the passengers had paid a good price for their holidays. I wonder if they thought the crew were made up of multiple twins and triplets as we were everywhere all the time.

At one stage I started coming down with it, but Leon the Ballroom barman was having none of that. He made me the most lethal cocktail of every hard spirit he could lay his hands on, lit it, put out the flames and said "Drink" I downed it in one and my nose and eyes ran like a sticky gooey tap. I felt like I was burning and choking all in one go but when the steam and fog cleared, so had my flu symptoms.

He should have patented it as now he'd be a millionaire.

By the time Easter arrived the flu had gone and even though we were all left quite weary, the idea of forth coming celebrations was enough to lift spirits again. The Greeks really get into Easter and that year we had two. One for us then the following week, one for them.

Good Friday (Ours) everything was shut in La Guaira, so I just headed down to the hospital for a chin wag with Anna and the nurses. They had a pretty hairy time with all the sickness. I think it was the first time ever the hospital had been full. Usually it's seasickness and the odd accident from a cook or engineer.

Saturday in Curacao, Anna and I asked for the afternoon off and with all the extra hours we'd put in they couldn't really refuse. We headed into town and met up with Gerda and Ginger who'd met some Dutch guys.

There is a Dutch navy base in Curacao and their ship, the Rotterdam was in port. Armed with fresh bread rolls stolen from the kitchen, peanut butter, chocolate hail and Heineken beer we really knew how to party. What a feast! When it was time to get back a couple of the guys offered us a lift, which we accepted.

We had a slight detour though. Who could resist a personal tour of a navy ship when it was offered. We couldn't stay long but it was fun.

Leaving Curacao always intrigued me. Our ship would slowly sail down a canal. The pontoon bridge would open for us and right up against the water's edge, Dutch style houses with people living in them could watch us float by. At the same time, we could look straight into their living rooms.

Whispers went around, had anyone seen Gerda? No one had since the afternoon and then looking down, zooming along besides us was a pilot boat with, yes, you've guessed it. Gerda. We ran down to the kitchen and yelled at them to open the door.

A rope ladder was thrown out and whilst we waited and waited with our hearts in our mouths. Gerda stuffed her wallet and bag into her shorts and bra, balanced on the edge of the pilot boat and just as the rope ladder got within reach, lunged for it and scrambled aboard.

She was met by cheering cooks and waiters and unfortunately the Staff Captain who dryly said, "Welcome Aboard".

Easter Sunday Angie had left a note on the mirror and a little gift for each of us.

At 12.45pm there was a message from the Chief Steward that I had to report to his office. Oh God what had I done wrong now, I wondered. But it was Ok. He gave me a box of Easter Bunnies and asked me to give one to each of the girls, even the nurses and hairdressers. He then said Happy Easter and planted a kiss. I asked why I was the chosen Easter Bunny and he said because I was the only one wishing all the passengers a Happy Easter. Bet I wasn't, he just wanted to give me a kiss.

Everything was going smoothly until the Thursday night, the dreaded cocktail party. I had the honour of serving the Captain's table yet again. With this gig, you don't just give them the same old watered-down bevies that the rest of the flock get. You take orders and have to remember who wants what. Numerous trips to the bar downstairs, where I am an unwelcome sight.

The barmen are frantically filling up glasses of premixed cocktails for the stewards and stewardess's trays in quicker than quick time.

Still once I'd got my load and headed back, the delicate manoeuvre of taking away the empty glass from one side and replacing with a full one the other side, all whilst balancing the slippery tray with stupidly cotton gloved hands.

I'd got right behind the Captain who was seated next to a rather fat lady when... **Bump!**

A steward hit my tray and the contents went careering straight down the Captain's back. If that wasn't bad enough, the compare had just that second announced the Captain's speech.

Like the true professional that he was, he simply stood up and walked to the stage totally ignoring the dripping mess that was the back of his jacket. Meanwhile, the Chief Steward, the other steward and I hastily cleaned up the mess. I live to tell the tale. I didn't have to walk the plank, but I did have to do the second sitting serving the Captain's table. A night I will never forget.

The Amerikanis, another ship in the Chandris family was in San Juan, so I think we did a whole crew swap. It's quite funny really. We all get a bit snooty about our own ship, finding fault with theirs. I didn't say this out loud though, but I thought the Amerikanis looked nicer than the Britanis, it was also smaller and had more of a cosy feel about it.

Thursday before Greek Easter we were in St Vincent and again I hopped in a taxi with some passengers. It had been another wonderful day, but all hell was breaking loose back on the Britanis.

Remember I told you I'd talk about Gerda a bit more later? Well there was an incident with her and Anna, both pissed to the eyeballs, sitting on the railings and about to plunge into the sea below.

We were anchored out and tenders took us to shore so theoretically, they should have been OK to go for a dip, BUT It wouldn't have been a smooth entry into the murky depths as the gangplank for the tenders was just below. They would have had a rather bumpy landing.

Luckily Annie noticed what they were up to and called for help. Leon the barman dropped the drink he was mixing ran and grabbed them off the railing.

They became vicious like wild creatures. Soon there were male crew everywhere trying to contain them. The nurse was called, she managed to inject Anna with something, and she flaked out but not so easy with Gerda. The needle went in, but she yanked it out. Some of the anaesthetic must have got into her blood stream because her knees began to buckle but it didn't hold her for long.

It took two Master at Arms, the Staff Captain a strong sailor and an apprentice officer to hold her before the nurse could inject her again. All four men had injuries consisting of scratches in the face, kicks in the groin and punches in the stomachs.

Gerda's bruises and black eyes were pretty spectacular to say the least. She was told not to report for work again until her black eye had returned to their normal red blood shot look we were all used to.

Good Friday Greek style saw a load of us heading to a restaurant in Caracas. The Greeks don't eat, meat, eggs, butter or cheese on this day but they still managed to spend a whopping $150 for lunch.

Greek Easter Sunday is the big celebration. At midnight Saturday/Sunday there was a massive party for the crew in the dining room. I headed down there about 1am, the party was in full swing and carried on all day.

They had a barbecue in the playroom and John was back in his Greek national dress dancing up a storm. Sunday night is always Greek night on the ship but this time it was sensational, even better than Greek National Day. Must remember this if ever I go on a holiday to Greece and want to party hard and wild.

Five days later it was Georges name day. The celebrations continue.

21 days to go and counting until we arrive back to England.

Nearly missed the ship in St Thomas through no fault of my own. There had been an aeroplane disaster. A Boeing 727 crashed into a service station instantly killing 27 people and injuring hundreds of others. Black plumes of smoke belched into the air and the roads were cut off. Ambulances and fire brigades rushed from every direction. Our taxi got us back just as the gangplank was lifting. This time no fines as we had a really good excuse.

May Day. Our last day in Curacao and everything was closed except the casino.

All the passengers always get four American quarters to spend at the Intercontinental Hotel's Casino. I also grabbed my free quarters and headed there as well. You can play any of the games, but I just had a go with the one-armed bandit but never won.

Sometimes when we went, we could swap our four coins for one giant dollar coin and put it in a giant one-armed bandit. It meant you only got one go but the machine looked pretty cool. Anyway, that's how we spent our last day there.

We only went to Antigua once. We wanted to make the most of it. I had the morning off with Annie from my cabin and Barbara a Cashier. After a quick look around town we headed for the beach and went horse riding. The horses were our tour guides and we loved where they took us. Up the top of the hill the view reminded me of the Australian bush except for the goats, chickens, cows and dogs that just roamed around.

Back down at the beach we met some guys who had a yacht and they were cruising the Caribbean. They invited us to join them and I seriously would have if the ship didn't keep our passports.

This cruise season was just about over, and I'd be looking for a new adventure soon anyway. Instead we opted for a mad ride in their hired Mini Moke.

There were 10 of us hanging on for dear life. We came across a privately-owned swimming pool which overlooked the beach. A middle-aged woman of about 30 liked the look of the yachting lads and invited us all in for a swim. Who could resist? None of us that's for sure.

We were served drinks and lapped up the attention. She was sad to see us go, well the guys anyway...I wonder if they had a second visit? But we had to get back to the ship and fast, I was now absent without leave...What could they do? Bite me!

Every island and port we left had a sad farewell. The ship would blow its horns, the tugs would respond with water jets and everyone waved us goodbye. So many places we'd seen and so many adventures and mishaps along the way. Now we were heading for the big smoke of New York. Goodbye little islands in the sun with your crystal-clear waters lapping up against white sandy beaches and warm sunshine. I didn't realise that one day in the not too distant future I'd be back.

New York 11th May 1976.

We've arrived and a stunning entrance we had. The sun was shining but it was a cold day. The Statue of Liberty stood proudly and the massive harbour docks with the imposing skyscrapers framing them took my breath away.

We were there for two whole days. Half the girls had the first morning off and I was one of those. I went ashore with Denise and her fellow Vasilis.

The city was quite overwhelming, and we just didn't know where to start. They really had yellow cabs and there really was an Italian neighbourhood. I know we wasted precious time and planning would have been a wonderful thing to do in hindsight, but we wandered.

As luck would have it, we stumbled across the Empire State Buildings, so up we went. Zoom, WOW! Who cares if your stomach is left on the floor many meters below? The twin towers were over there and compared to the beauty of the old Art Deco buildings, they just looked like Lego blocks.

Now we were getting into the whole tourist thing. Catch a cab to The Statue of Liberty. This massive green giant. We get inside the pedestal then take the lift up as high as we can. The rest of the way is by climbing the steps. Like any museum, there is always so much to read and see, but we act like bogan tourists and scramble about trying to absorb as much as possible in the shortest amount of time.

A yellow cab back to the ship, I meet Les who's been patiently waiting on the docks for me and I'd totally forgotten all about him. We grab a few parting words before I have to rush back, get changed and become a stewardess again. What a horrible person I was. I probably would have had a better time with him showing me around if I had only remembered. Oh well.

Passing the baton to the girls waiting to get ashore we quickly gave them a run down on what we'd seen and done.

I worked until just gone midnight and then off a group of us went to a nightclub. Back by 5am and at 9am I was back at work. We actually had a morning cocktail party. That wasn't a massive one though. Just for travel agents and such like so not too taxing and an easy clean up, still weird though.

The afternoon was spent shopping and then back for the Christening of a Chandris grandson. The Greek Orthodox priest did the service and then another cocktail party, buffet and show with free drinks all night.

Finally free at 1am we grab a cab and shoot off to a disco. It closed 10 minutes after we arrived so back to bed.

As we were leaving the next morning, I'm sure I saw Lady Liberty wave.

The Atlantic crossing was smooth and it took me two full days to recover from my tiredness.

Here we go again, many farewells, tears and kisses. Promises to meet again and possibly they will all get broken.

Who knew what was just around the corner?

Oh, and as for David the tall, dark handsome Welsh guy? Well we parted company a couple of months back and I've been with Yannis the grumpy 36-year-old man who never did get a punch in the nose, but he did get something, wink, wink.

## Chapter 19
# Aussie Visa
## What a Kerfuffle

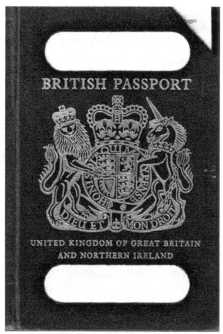

*Old British passport*

Good old Bill was there waiting for me again in Southampton. He took me back to his family home and after a phone call to my Uncle I went and stayed with John and Betty again for a few days.

Little Blackie was a bit of a nutcase. If I wanted a bath the fire had to be lit so the water would heat up. Blackie's new game is to take smouldering hot coals straight out of the fire and drop them on the multi scorch-marked hearth rug. You dare not leave her in the room alone or the house might burn down.

John and Betty always made me feel so welcome and never missed an opportunity to take me to something uniquely English.

This time they took me to the Hertfordshire County Show. The cows were as big as elephants and all looked happy. They had pig racing (I hope that meant they ran away from any carving knives), Welly Wangling (Seeing how far your Wellington boot can be flung) and all sorts of local food and booze.

It was a great day out but a massive traffic jam when we tried to leave. I had the back seat of the car to myself, so I thought it was a good idea to have a snooze. John didn't think that was a good idea and every time I got comfy, he slammed the breaks on, and I fell off the seat. Obviously didn't have seat belts back then and he thought it was hilarious. I did too to tell you the truth.

As you can imagine not only had I been gathering up souvenirs and presents for my friends and family I also had a whole mountain of excess stuff that I wanted to keep for myself, only thing for it was to organise a trunk load of goodies to be sent back home to Australia. Easier said than done I was to find out.

There was paperwork by the reams, insurance, delivery people and everyone wanted to be paid. After a few false starts and plenty of quids leaving my purse my trunk and one large suitcase were on the way to Melbourne leaving the customs palaver to be dealt with by my long-suffering parents. My aunt was given a whole suitcase of clothes and gifts and so were the Green family.

Ahh, that's better, a lighter load.

One of the girls I shared a cabin with on the Britanis was living in

Chiswick, so I bunked in with her for a couple of days whilst all this was going on. This made the multiple journeys to London a whole lot quicker.

I wanted to change my American Dollars and most of my English Pounds into traveller's cheques but came across another hurdle. They wanted proof that the English money was mine and that I'd paid tax. Well I hadn't paid tax because I'd earned it working on the ship, so then I had to open a British bank account, deposit the money before I could withdraw it again and convert it into traveller's cheques.

Another little obstacle to put a spanner in the works was the new law of return visas to Australia. I had a British passport which was a good thing for travelling around Britain, Europe and just about everywhere else but as of the 1st January 1975 I needed a re- entry visa if I ever wanted to go home. It had never entered my head that they might not want me back especially as most of my life and education and family and animals and EVERYTHING was over there. When I applied and got my British passport back in early 1974 the idea of a return visa wasn't even mentioned.

Oh well a trip to Australia House in London and a stamp in my passport would sort that out I thought. Boy was I ever wrong. I was told it could take weeks as they had to write to Canberra, and they needed to keep my passport whilst all that was going on. Well I planned to be in England for a little while but only a very little while. The world was waiting for me.

I filled out loads of paperwork and left my passport with them but said I might need to come and get it back soon.

Hmm, was that a rye look on the officious looking clerk's face I wondered?

My friend Doreen was now doing her nurses training and invited me to stay in the nurse's home for the weekend. This was great fun and I also got to meet her new beau, Julius, and all his family. They are all either medical people or training to be medical people. Julius was training to be a doctor. I must have made the right impression because I was invited to stay with them the next weekend.

On Friday 4th June the Britanis docked at Tilbury so I went along to see Yannis. He was hoping to get off the ship on the 18th and we were going to travel around Europe together but unfortunately, they wouldn't let him off yet. The crew can feel quite trapped sometimes. You have to stay on for the full term of your contract because they keep your passport which means if you jump ship you're stuffed. In Yannis's case even two weeks' notice wasn't enough.

Sharing myself around and trying not to be too much of a burden on family I asked Gina and David if I could come and stay for about a week. Luckily, they said yes. My cousin Stephen and I would go for walks each night sometimes up to nine miles but usually only about four or five miles, we both enjoy the countryside and I also enjoyed his company.

Paul is his younger brother and was on school holidays, so he came into London with me a few times. I forgot he was only sixteen and we went and saw a stupid Carry On movie which he was legally too young for, but we didn't tell his mum and had a good laugh anyway.

When I stayed at anyone's home, I tried to always make myself useful and that was usually doing the cooking. The women of the house liked the idea and it gave them a break. I also liked cooking. Gina was especially pleased with this arrangement as cooking has never been her favourite pastime.

One time she was out, and I made a concoction for dinner but didn't know what to call it. Paul was studying French, so we decided to give this dish a French name to make it sound appetising. We came up with the name, *'Tout sauf les chaussures'*. Which means, 'Everything but shoes '. Paul and I couldn't stop laughing when they asked what was for dinner.

I was in a dilemma; I couldn't keep free loading on friends and family forever. It was either find a job and a flat, go back and work on the ship (that's what Yannis wanted me to do) or travel solo.

The following weekend I went and stayed with Julius's family and we had a brilliant time. Summer in the English countryside means fairs every weekend and we found them.

We ate Candy Floss, had many a sickly ride on whizzy things and acted like the mad children that we were. I also told them of my unsettledness, and they seemed to be unanimous in thinking I should travel solo.

Great, so having my mind made up for me I rang a few travel agencies and found something that looked quite interesting. Problem was, I needed my passport back.

Australia House handed back my passport still without a visa stamp but said they would keep all the paperwork on file for the next time I applied for it. Bloody Hell!! Bureaucracy at height.

June the 18th arrived and with great trepidation I went to tell Yannis my decision. The trip that I'd planned was for six and a half weeks, he said he could wait that long for me and by then he may be able to leave the ship. I didn't want to tell him that I'd probably be broke by that time and have to find work again. Being the coward that I was and still am, I kept quiet about that.

## Chapter 20
# Top Deck
## An Unfortgettable Adventure

*Snot, the Top Deck bus I toured Europe in*

The travel agency was in Fulham and the lady who sold me the tour assured me that it would be 'The Trip of a Lifetime'.

I had the very last seat for the 23rd June departure. It wasn't actually camping in the traditional sense, but I would need to take a sleeping bag and the bare necessities in either a plastic bag or laundry bag. WOW! That's living life on the edge! It cost 225 British Pounds for the actual trip plus six pounds a week for the food kitty and three pounds fifty for insurance in case I got sick.

The Itinerary was: Paris, Pont du Gard, Antibes, Monaco, Pisa, Florence, Rome, Pompeii, Corfu, Igoumenitsa, Patras, Athens, Greek Islands, Platamon, Skopje, Titograd, Dubrovnik, Split, Zadar, Venice, Salzburg, Munich, Lucern, Interlaken, Heidelberg, Amsterdam and Bruges.

All these places and all these weeks on a .... wait for it....Double Decker Bus!. The company was called Top Deck.

Well with an overstuffed laundry bag and a sleeping bag I made my way to the departure point and met up with twenty total strangers. I made number twenty-one.

The bus wasn't anything like the one Cliff Richard had on his **"*Summer Holiday*** 'This was dirty orange and cream coloured with the number 69 in the direction window. It did have a door that could close though, not like the normal double deckers that you can just jump on. Inside it had some bench seating as well as a sink and stove and cupboards. Upstairs was where most of us were to sleep. They had triple bunks on both sides with a narrow aisle down the middle. The seats downstairs also became beds. Your allotted bunk with a mattress was also your cupboard.

Everyone had to take turns in cooking and washing up. They had giant tins of spaghetti and coffee and other stuff, but we were told they stop along the way and buy fresh food and of course there was nothing stopping us buying our own food.

I was partnered with a girl called Carolyn for our domestic duties and she seemed nice. The courier was Mike, the driver was Kevin and they were both scruffy Aussies. In fact, we all were either Aussies or

Kiwis and most of us were in our twenties with a couple in their thirties.

Carolyn and I were to experience the joys of washing up duty for the first three days.

We drove to the edge of England, boarded a ferry, got over to the edge of France and headed for Paris. It was already hot and we traipsed all over the tourist spots. I loved Paris instantly and Carolyn and I seemed to be of the same mind set.

A man drew my portrait and gave it to me for nothing, well I was supposed to meet him for a drink later. I didn't turn up, besides the picture wasn't all that good. I looked about twelve years old.

We climbed to the top of the Arc de Triumph and looking down we saw our bus with the word SNOT written in orange paint on its roof. I asked Mike the courier about that and he said that was the buses name. Tasteful!

The French drivers were terrifying when you watch them whizzing around the Etoile, luckily you can get to the Arc de Triumph from under the road.

We saw all the usual sights and climbed everything you needed to climb, had our photos taken with a couple of gendarmes, got chased by some black guys which was terrifying and finally found the bus and jumped on for refuge.

That night we headed for a camping ground and as it was way too hot to sleep like a sardine inside, I took my sleeping bag and mattress and slept under the stars.

The sun rose early and so did I. 5.30am actually so it gave me time to have a shower, wash my hair and clothes and even make twenty one breakfasts whilst the others staggered down to ready themselves for the day. My clothes were even dry before we took off again.

Once we left Paris it was a full day's drive to Pont de Gard. Supposed to be anyway but the bus over heated and also needed refuelling.

Stuck on the side of the road Kevin and Mike started pulling the engine to pieces. After a while they seemed happy enough with whatever they did and put the engine back together again.

Finally getting to the highway...BANG!! The bus ground to a halt. Everything got pulled out again, a lot of swearing mixing with grease and oil before hitting the road again. It was quite funny really. Our sixteen-year-old bus doesn't look a day over twenty-five.

Finally reaching the camp site at Pont du Gard only to find it was full and we were sent on our way, obviously it's a first in first served arrangement. They did find another camp site and this one looked nicer anyway. It had a bar and everyone lobbed in there and stayed until about three in the morning.

The sun woke me even earlier the next morning, so saying hello to a bullfrog on the way to the shower I was all washed and ready for the day before anyone else surfaced.

Sleeping in a cabin on the ship with absolutely no natural light must have smothered my brain because I simply couldn't sleep once the sun was up anymore.

The trip took us past ancient Roman viaducts, we stocked up with fresh produce at Avignon market, it rained in St Raphael which kept the engine of the bus cool, so small mercies I guess besides the beaches didn't look that special, they looked like a lot of the English beaches only with more boats and higher prices.

Antibes camp site had a swimming pool which we all dived in. The beach was pretty close and as there were two other bus tour groups a beach party was arranged.

Everyone collected wood and a big bonfire was made. They all brought loads of booze and the night turned wild. Next morning most people had sore heads and were green around the gills. The drive to Monte Carlo was quietly subdued.

Monaco is a pocket of pure indulgence as far as I could make out. A pretty principality with its own castle that the royal family live in, a deep bay with floating mini ships they call yachts and an expensive casino where the real money gets laundered, I imagine. They have their own police force, stamps and even an army which consists of twelve men. All this in a mere three hundred acres. It is said that when the family dies out this little dot of a country will all belong to France.

The casino in Monte Carlo had a ten-franc entry fee and ten franc minimum per bet. Far too expensive for me and most of the others so we headed for a plunge in the overly salty sea before going to a bar.

At midnight we entered Italy. The customs guys were so laid back but were especially interested in the girls who had gone to bed. They called us Kangaroos and after cheekily checking our passports and anything else that caught their eyes, we entered that fine country without any problems.

Except of course the bus, which had to make yet another stop on the side of the road where we stayed the night. The engine had cooled sufficiently by morning.

The guys on the bus decided to initiate all the females in the traditional Italian male greeting. They kept pinching us on the bum.

I desperately needed a wee, but no facilities were anywhere around. Luckily a beach was just over a wall and below some beach huts. Easy enough to scale the walls, scramble over the roofs of the huts, lower myself down onto a table and *Voula* a secret area to relieve myself in. Only problem was getting back up to the roadside in pitch blackness. It was a bit hazardous but eventually made it.

Next morning the bus actually started. We drove all the way to a station where we could change our money. Pisa was the next official stop, but poor old SNOT decided she needed a few more rests along the way especially when she was asked in fact pleaded to ascend a hill. A few more glugs of water and she made it.

The tower really does lean and the stone steps are worn down at quite an angle inside. I climbed the circle of steps that are also very slippery but made it to the top without falling out the bell tower.

On my postcard home I wrote;

"I'm gunna haveta lose weight, I stood in here and it nearly toppled".

Field of Miracles is the English translation of this small square consisting of four buildings. Apart from the usual tourists having photos taken *Holding Up* the tower, there were also stall holders selling souvenirs as well as the devout having a little pray. This is where we sampled our first real Italian pizza. It wasn't round but square and they just cut a slab of it and handed it to us on a bit of paper. Cheap and tasty. Yum.

The campsite that night was in Florence which wasn't too far away but when we got there another Top Deck mob was making itself known. They were a real rowdy foul-mouthed lot so instead of being excited about meeting up with them we were all more excited that they were just about to leave.

The loos in this site were the squatting ones. It's a balancing act and I was terrified of falling into the hole. The showers were also built for the perving eye as well. The doors were like saloon doors in Western films, short and swinging with no locks. Needless to say, none of us females lingered.

The city of Florence made up for the inadequacies of the camp site though. The marble cathedral was awe inspiring. The statue of David was fabulous to see in real life, but the other statues were just as glorious.

Carolyn, Sarina and I wandered off on our own through the markets and I bought myself a pair of shorts. Packing only a few essentials meant running out of clean clothes quite quickly and I was getting sick of having to do my washing every time the bus pulled into a camp site.

I think disposable clothing would be the better way to travel in situations like this. Don't wash 'em.... chuck 'em!

I remember writing home and saying I wonder why all the Italians moved to Australia when their own country is so beautiful, no wonder they got homesick.

In the evening we were all going to a disco but once again our bus let us down. Poor old Kevin spent the entire day up to his eyeballs in cogs, sprockets, bits of string and chewing gum. I think that may have been the problem.....these were the buses main working parts.

Mike suggested we take the local bus, so we all headed for the bus stop. I stuck out my thumb and Hey Presto, got a lift instantly. Four of us piled into the car so the others all did the same.

I was dancing with Mike to start with but when he went to get a drink an Italian guy became my next partner. *The Bump* dance craze was still the happening thing and this guy Bumped me so hard I went flying. Then he picked me up and started swinging me around. What did he think I was? Pizza Dough?

Another Aussie tour group turned up. They were the Contiki crowd and between us we ruled that joint. When the disco finished, everyone made tracks to a little late-night pizza shop. The poor proprietors nearly had a heart attack when they saw these two groups of rampaging, starving, sweaty Aussies coming towards them.

The Contiki bus group squashed up and gave all us Top Deck mob a lift back to the campsite.

Mike was actually quite drunk and kept picking me up and carrying me about. I think this was some kind of Courier Mating Ritual. Which I didn't appreciate. Luckily, he didn't drop me. Finally, he fell asleep sprawled across my lap. I wriggled away and went to bed.

Rome. WOW! I could see why they call it the eternal city. Even with the modern roads, cars and buildings the ancient city still shines through. It was a bit hard to see the statue of Romulus and Remus with the She Wolf at first but as we neared the city itself, we could see it. The Colosseum is a real ruin and apparently there was talk about restoring it back to its original grandeur. Luckily, the people were dead against it. The magic would have been lost.

Kevin got poor old Snot safely to the campsite after a quick peek around and then we headed off in small groups again.

Carolyn and I ate pizza on the steps of the Church of Trinita De Monti wandered through markets where local artists make and sell their wares. Went inside the Pantheon which looked every day of its 2000years old on the outside the inside was breathtaking, all still original and well preserved

At the Trevi fountain I stood facing away and threw a French franc into the water over my shoulder. The legend says if you throw a coin into the fountain you will return to Rome. I will probably return as a French person now.

That night we ate out using 1000Lira each from the kitty. That was OK because a meal cost between 700Lira to 1000Lira. One Australian dollar approximately.

We parked outside the Forum and being tight fisted most of us chose to take photos from the outside because it cost 2000Lira to enter and walk around but we could clearly see everything from the other side of the fence.

Before leaving Rome, I walked down the Roman catacombs. How creepy was that? Underground burial chambers with skulls and bones all on display. It was very interesting, but I was worried about getting lost in the labyrinth of the dead.

The Appium Way was the first road to lead to Rome and it's still there today, complete with chariot tracks. We actually drove some of the way on it. The ancient huge Roman baths were on the top of the hill. Men used to bathe and then go down the hill and have their wicked way with women. They still do because the bottom of the hill is the prostitute area. The prostitutes have little fire lamps at night to advertise that they are open for business.

I'm pleased to say that none of the guys on our bus ventured down that hill.

A quick visit to the Vatican just happened to be July 4th so the Pope popped out onto the balcony and wished all the Americans a happy Bicentenary.

On our way out of Rome I actually fell asleep and woke up by the Abbey of Montecassino. The drive is usually only just over an hour but not for us. Snot struggled her way and unless I slept through everyone pushing her, we actually managed to ascend this mountain.

The views from up there was worth waking up for. It was also a couple of the guys turns to make lunch so tinned spaghetti and garlic bread seems appropriate. It was actually quite nice; the surroundings made a difference as well.

From there we headed to Naples. The bus was parked. The guys headed off for a beer. For some reason we girls all decided it was letter writing time. Unfortunately, the locals must have thought we were a travelling brothel. They constantly pestered us by knocking on the windows and calling out. We closed the curtains but that did nothing, in fact I think that made them really think we were tasty treats. Eventually a rather hefty Kiwi born Polish lass swore at them so forcefully that they backed off. The power of words, even if you have no idea what was said.

Our men returned and we headed to Pompeii. This was a bit of a letdown to tell the truth. A lot of the place had been boarded up and only a few exhibits were on display. However, what we could see was awe-inspiring. The little dog that had been caught in the ash fallout from the volcano still haunts me.

We next drove to Brindisi where we were supposed to catch a ferry to Corfu. Problem was. Yes, there was another problem but this time it was the ferry. It had caught fire and now there was a huge backlog of hot grumpy people who had to either stay in their cars and try to sleep or go to an hotel somewhere. I could just imagine the hotel owners rubbing their hands together and whacking up the prices, or is that too cynical?

We were sort of lucky because the bus was also our beds, kitchen and entertainment room. Just had to pop out to find a loo and as for showers to clean our smelly. sticky, hot bodies...it had to wait.

Carolyn and I were now rostered on to do the cooking. Breakfast was easy, Cornflakes and toast. Lunch was salad with cold meats, dinners were Steak and Kidney pies found in the storage cupboard that just needed heating up and fresh tomatoes and zucchinis, finishing with fruit salad and cream.

We had gone for a drive to kill time while waiting for the ferry and this just happened to be when I was digging through the cupboards looking for inspiration for the night's meal. As the bus turned a corner, CRASH! Down came a large bottle of vinegar and met with my head. I was a bit stunned as I sat there on the floor. One of the girls was a nurse and declared that I would live, so now I sported a rather colourful bump on my forehead.

Eventually another ferry was called into action and the cars started driving on. That of course is far too easy. Our bus was too tall as they found out when the top crunched into the opening of the hold. Next trick, let the tyres down, put planks of wood under her and gently persuade her in. Nope, still too tall. Well after re inflating the tyres and a lot of quick thinking the bus and us were going our separate ways. This was quite terrifying because if anything happened to Snot, we would be left high and dry. It was midnight before we set sail but one consolation, there were showers on board.

The ferry was rocking away. I dropped the soap, bent down to pick it up and bumped my head on the basin, dropped the soap again and bumped again. Then I had a bump on the front and the back of my head, once more and I'd probably kill my silly self.

Anyway, we were all delighted in being clean and sweet smelling once again. We met at the bar and worried in unison about our beloved and troublesome home away from home until eventually we had fitful sleeps in the world's most uncomfortable chairs. Next morning at daylight we were excited to see the barge carrying Snot keeping up with us and we all got to land at about the same time.

A great sigh of relief from all of us when we were reunited on the beautiful island of Corfu even though it was belting down with rain. Kevin gave us a quick tour of the island before heading to the camping ground and by that time the sun was shining.

A large pear tree overhung the driveway and as our bus passed under, we managed to knock off a few hundred slightly under ripe fruit. We all gathered them up and I stewed a huge pot full for dessert later. Once we'd parked, I made everyone some lunch before we split and went our own separate ways.

Some of them hired mopeds, some went to the beach and some just chilled out.

It was great to hear that familiar language of the Greeks that I had become quite accustom to. Still couldn't speak it but understood if I was being sworn at, told they loved me or to Man the Lifeboats.

Greek dancing lessons were on offer that night, but it turned into the usual disco. First, I danced with a Yank, then another then the tallest Dutch guy I'd ever met. I had to reach up really high to put my hands on his shoulders and when my neck was getting cricked from looking up all the time, I just had to navel watch.

Mike was getting a bit peeved and asked me to come outside to join with the Top Deck group but when I did go outside it was only him. He sarcastically asked if I was enjoying myself and my answer was in the affirmative. Three Danish guys who I'd never met overheard the conversation and each one came up and kissed me goodnight and said they'd had a wonderful time. Silly buggers.

We had a couple of days in Corfu and that allowed us a bit more time than a quick peek. Some of us in the campsite, not just the Top Deck mob, hired a boat and cruised around the island until we found the perfect spot to anchor. I was quite content to sunbathe but that never happened because within minutes I was chucked overboard. Everyone else jumped in so I hoped there would be a lifesaver amongst them if I needed it. Later we headed into town for fish and chips.

Our last lazy day on Corfu saw me doing my washing.

We later took the ferry to Athens, this time without incident.

We were in for a long drive and kept our fingers firmly in a locked crossed position that the bus would actually make it. Our first official stop was Patras then we hesitantly continued on to see the Corinth Canal. We made it and rested the bus, gave her a drink and some fuel while we explored and marvelled at this man-made chasm.

Then on to Athens. It wasn't without incident but that must be getting boring reading by now so I'm going to skip it.

The campsite in Athens is muddy and the showers either flood or don't work, but they have a swimming pool and a disco plus a wonderful city to check out.

We all headed to the Acropolis together before doing our usual split up sightseeing. I headed for the flea markets and found some lovely souvenirs. I wanted to see the changing of the guards and was told it happened at 2 o'clock but when I got there at 5 to 2 it had already happened which was disappointing.

The next day was an early one. We drove down to Piraeus in time for the ferry that left at 8am. This time the bus stayed behind. Leaving with our sleeping bags, clothes and bathers we boarded for a three-hour trip to the island of Poros. We ate sandwiches for lunch and then Lyn, Lindsey, Dianne, Cathy and I headed for the town and bought beach mats.

At the beach dinghies could be hired along with their owners. Our dinghy headed left; the others went right. It didn't matter because all the beaches were lovely and after sunbathing and swimming there for a while we got back into the boats and met up with the others. Feeling salt encrusted from the swimming the only fresh water tap we could find was on the side of a café, so we took it in turns to splash ourselves down

Time alone was something I was craving. All these months spent with so many people. This island seemed to offer the solitude that I desired. The shoreline was rocky, so I climbed up to the road and followed it for a while. I saw what I thought to be old ruins but on closer inspection I could see they were inhabited by turkeys, chickens and menagerie of other animals and old people. Looking over the distant harbour I could see a lonely house on a small island, it looked so peaceful, beyond that a hydrofoil going past. Three things from one vantage point all from different eras.

Off the side of the road there was a rough track which looked like it hadn't been trodden on for quite some time. The further up the mountain I climbed, the track seemed to disappear into wild scrub and prickles.

This was an impromptu climb and I only had thin sandals on my feet which meant that a prickly bush and I got closely associated when a large thorn lodged in my foot. I waited for a lion to come along and pluck it out and be my friend for life, but alas that didn't happen, I just had to pull it out myself.

Next I came across giant spider webs criss crossing like barbed wire from one spiky bush to another. If I wasn't phobic about spiders, I might have marvelled at their beautiful structures but as I didn't want to meet the architects of these fine things, I had to divert through the undergrowth for another route only to be attacked by flying insects.

Once I crested the mountain it was simple pleasures that I took in the beauty of the ruggedness of this terrain. Twenty minutes later I thought about the decent. This time I could sort of see where to go and it was much easier until I came upon a fence.

Damn, I hadn't seen that from up high and the only way out was to climb up and over. Luckily the owners were friendly and watched in amazement as this T-shirted and shorts clad girl who appeared from nowhere sauntered through their back yard and onto the road.

Meeting up with everyone a while later we had dinner in a small café and then unrolled our sleeping bags and slept right there on the beach.

Next morning it was a wash at the tap at the side of the café, pack up, climb into dinghies where breakfast was served to us on trestle tables in town whilst we waited for another ferry to take us to Hydra, another island.

WOW! Hydra was the most beautiful place I'd ever seen. All the buildings and even the stone paths were whitewashed and gleaming clean. No cars come on to this island, they have beautiful little donkeys who help them with the carting and they just seem to know exactly where to go because once they are loaded up nobody leads them, they just go to wherever they are meant to go, I think.

Al, Peter and I took ourselves off on a photographic journey and were offered freshly squeezed lemon drinks from the café we bought our lunch from. We eventually met up with the rest after taking a little boat trip to a wonderful beach, had a swim and then in all too short a time we had to get back for the return ferry to Poros and finally Piraeus where Snot and Kevin were patiently waiting for us.

Back on the road again this time we were heading for Platamon but as that was hours away we had a petrol station stop in Thermopylae where we all piled out and had a wash and a wee a good look around the hot springs and the monument of Leonidas and Spartans. It's funny to think that the Greek waiters and stewards on the ships that I've worked on are descendants from these guys.

Platamon was a two day stop over so as usual it was time to do my washing. Oh, I wish I'd had disposable clothes. Once the boring chores were finished Cathy and I hiked to the castle way on top of the hill. A little church had its own little Greek Orthodox priest who greeted us and then offered us some bread which we accepted before having a wander around the ruins.

Deciding to come down the short way and nearly breaking our necks, I understand why they make roads but sometimes it's more fun to live dangerously. The beach here is one of the largest in Greece so we made full use of it.

In the evening everyone had headed to the bar but just before Cathy and I went, four Yugoslavians came and asked if they could use our cooker. We saw no harm in it and for payment they made us Turkish coffee and then read our coffee cups. I am pleased to say that their predictions have been correct so far.

I was to have a good life ahead of me.

Later at the bar Cathy and met a couple of guys and we stayed chatting to them until the wee small hours of the morning.

It was another full day on the road when we headed for Yugoslavia with about one hundred stops for either a bus engine cool down or a quick pee behind a bush. We passed peasant women in national dress working in fields, young children rounding and herding up huge cattle with only a stick, a yell and masses of confidence. Lots of donkey carts that we passed, or they passed us along the road. It was slow progress and we had another night stop on the side of the road.

Early next morning, I mean really early about 4.30am, Mike took the wheel to give Kevin a break, so I sat up the front with him and I'm so glad I got to see this sight.

Peasants walking or in their donkey carts by the hundred leading cows, pigs or barrows of fruit and vegetables on the way to the market. By the time we got to the market everyone was waking up Mike bought our fresh supplies, and everyone headed for the loos.

These were even worse than the worst ones we've used so far. I'm not going into detail about them but just let me say that a pair of gumboots would have been handy.

Carolyn and I were back on washing up duty and we did this whilst driving along. The scenery was fantastic with great big rocky mountains and beautiful lush fields. Those with the added abundance of peasants made us feel like we'd gone back in time, at least a couple of hundred years.

There were many little freshwater wells along the way and at one of these whilst filling up a bucket of water, over the hill came some strange feral looking men. They ran at the bus and pushed their hands in through the windows grabbing at us. They looked like "*One Flew Over The Cuckoo's Nest* extras. Absolutely terrifying, even Kevin and Mike got spooked so we drove on quickly away.

It was another scorcher of a day and the sun was going down before we and our bus with its steaming engine rolled into the campsite near Dubrovnik.

Dubrovnik is a beautiful medieval walled city with large gates and a drawbridge. No cars and millions of steps and expensive unfortunately. I had a cable car ride to the top of the mountain; from there you can see many little islands and the views were magnificent.

Down at sea level the old stones and boulders that have fallen away over the centuries have become home to many sea urchins in the shallows. People were plucking them up and putting them into baskets for eating later on. Sea urchins and bare feet are a hazard I didn't want to encounter so just sitting on the rocks was all I was game to do.

That evening we were all heading into the old town for a national meal. Our old bus stayed at the campsite and we all made our own way. Some caught the local bus in, some walked, and some hadn't left there all day. Arrangements had been made to meet up at the restaurant.

I was ready early so plonked myself down on a wall while I waited for the others. A creepy looking guy came up and started chatting to me. He told me he was always alone and wanted me to come back with him to his place, alone, later. Um, No thanks. His name was Demol, but it sounded more like Evol and then he tried to put his arms around me.... time to go and meet the rest of the gang!!! YIKES!

Dinner was delicious but the atmosphere with the group was

leaving a nasty taste in my mouth. A divide was beginning to happen between the happy campers. Only three of us remained neutral so hopefully a full-blown war wouldn't descend.

To add fuel to the fire a thunderstorm was brewing and by the time we were due to leave, the heavens had opened. No chance to stay in the town at night as the gates closed so we made a mad dash to the bus stop and caught the wrong bus. Eventually getting back to camp all looking like drowned rats, steam was beginning to charge out of ears. What to do? I made everyone hot drinks and then buggered off to bed.

Next morning breakfast was eaten, dishes washed, and everything repacked all in stony silence. Oh well.

Back on the road. Our bus was too tall to go through the usual road tunnel so we had a diversion around the docks. To my absolute delight I saw not one but two Chandris ships. I'd never seen either of them before but that give away white cross on a blue funnel had my heart fluttering. One was the Fiorita and the other Bon Vivant and believe it or not I knew four of the crew.

They were looking at this strange bus driving slowly around the dock road and I was scanning all the faces I could see; it was magic when we recognised each other. Unfortunately, we weren't allowed to stop so mad calling out and kisses blown was all that we could manage. This lifted my spirits to great heights.

If the others on the bus wanted to be grumpy; well let them!

Everyone seemed to be catching colds. Another night of thunderstorms which lit up the night sky, the bus had broken down again which kept us cabin bound didn't help the situation until one of the guys started singing silly songs and then we all joined in and the nasty mood was broken. Hooray.

The next morning Kevin took off into town to get a spare part. He was due back by 9.30am or 10am at the latest but 5pm came and went and still no Kevin. The days without mobile phones, we just had to sit and wait and hope he hadn't been abducted by aliens.

Finally, he turned up with a tale to tell. He'd missed the first bus and the next wasn't until 1pm, so he bought himself some breakfast and decided to hitch hike. The first and only lift came within a few minutes but only took him about 5 km. He was unsuccessful after that and had to walk the rest of the way. Another night on the roadside because he was too knackered to even think about fixing the bus, so we all wandered off and found a bar.

I met a boy and his father who were German and couldn't speak much English, but they bought me a Turkish coffee and with sign language we were getting along just fine. Then a group of Dutch guys turned up and that made things easier because they could speak German and English (Oh, what a clever country these Dutch people come from) and a merry team we became.

When the bar closed everyone came back to the bus and sat outside along the sea wall. One of the Dutch guys said he'd just got back from Curacao. My ears pricked up. He was in the Dutch navy. I sat closer and asked which ship he was on. It was the Rotterdam and he knew the guys that I met a few months ago. In fact, he was there when I was. Brilliant. What a small world!

Next morning Kevin, Mike and by now most of the other guys had become apprentice bus mechanics popped in its new part, chucked out the old broken bit (you can tell I know a lot about engines)and off we went to Split.

It's a pretty city but seemed very poor. We only stayed for a few hours and then drove on until dinner time. I can't remember who the cooks and cleaners were I just know it wasn't Carolyn and I again. We'd parked opposite a café and even though we ate our own food we used their loos. The headlights needed fixing now but the guys decided to stay just where we were and maybe tackle it another time.

Next day we drove for ages and stopped for a break in a little town that nobody knew the name of. It was good to get out of the bus for a while and stretch our legs. The sea next to the road was crystal clear and teaming with baby fish.

Zadar was supposed to be our next stop but as we were actually making good time and the bus was behaving itself, we carried on towards Venice instead.

I bet I missed out on some amazing place and experience. Oh well, nothing I could do about it. We crossed the border at 8pm and boy you could tell the difference between the Yugoslavs and the Italian custom men. The Yugo's were serious, efficient and just got on with the job, the Italians first noticed the number of the bus (69) joked and winked, came aboard and tasted the cooking that was happening at the time, carried on a bit and then let us pass. We reached the campsite on the mainland close to Venice at 1am.

*Rain, rain go away, come again another day.*

But it didn't go away, it hung around and in fact it belted down harder before turning into hail stones.

Kevin drove the bus right up to the ferry terminal and we clambered aboard then reaching Venice we made a mad dash for shelter and all bought ridiculous looking plastic raincoats for an exorbitant cost. It was obviously the main fashion item here because everyone was sporting one in many various colours.

The post office had two letters from home for me which was something I was looking forward to. Then off to the bank to change money again before hitting the shops. We could be here all day as long as we were back on the bus by 6pm. Such lovely things to buy and so many places to get lost in. Some of the walls of the buildings look close enough to kiss each other and many an umbrella ballet happened in these narrow lane ways.

When I only have a short time and there is so much to see and do. I always seem to manage to waste time and miss things. This had to be a place to come back and experience properly one day. It is so pretty even in the rain and it didn't smell as much as I thought it would, but I wouldn't want to swim here. Probably get run over by a gondola anyway.

The campsite had wonderful hot showers which never ran out. Pure luxury. Clean hair clean me and clean clothes, oh for the small pleasures in life.

There was another double decker bus here. It wasn't a manky looking thing like ours. It had class. The guy who owned it kept it in tip top condition and travelled anywhere he felt like. He had paying passengers who had to go along with his plans. He advertised each year where he planned to go and if anyone wants to share the costs and he likes them, that's what they would do. *Cool.*

Austria, Germany, Austria then back to Germany. That's what we did for the next few days. The scenery was so beautiful I didn't want to blink and miss anything. I felt like I was in a fairy-tale land. We had many photo stops along the way as well as the usual tourist traipsing, money changing and shopping, but I don't know about the others, I was beginning to feel quite grubby in these beautifully clean places.

Munich was our next two-night stop. You had to pay for the hot water in the showers and there was no way I could cope with a cold one, especially as the temperature was dropping. It was a fun and easy place to get around and didn't take me too long to understand the rail and tram systems. The town square or Marienplatz has a musical clock which I found out when people started to gather and stare upwards. Glad I didn't miss that.

At the campsite there is another Top Deck group and we are all meeting in the beer hall later in the evening. I went and had a look during the day, it didn't look that exciting, but when we all turned up at night the place was buzzing. Serving women in national costume were carrying twelve full steins at a time. Six in each hand. I picked one up and that was heavy enough. They would come to your table and yell something like "oomph!' and slide and plonk them down at the same time. They even had giant pretzels. That was what I was most interested in.

Of course, there was a competition. The girls had to drink two steins to receive a badge or pendant and the guys had to drink four. Doesn't sound much but each stein holds two and a half pints and as a person who doesn't even drink alcohol, I accepted the challenge.

It took me about an hour to get through the first one and before the empty glass touched the table another was placed in my hand. It was a struggle, but I managed it and then headed for the toilet.

I wasn't sick but I weed pure Munich beer. By the time I found my way back to the table my legs had turned against me. They refused to go in the direction I wanted them to. Someone grabbed me and took me outside for some fresh air and that's all I remember of that night. The bus didn't make it back to the campsite that night either, it was still parked at the same place where we were dropped off the evening before. I was on board, so some kind sole had taken me home I have no idea who.

Next morning bedraggled and in desperate need of a wee plus a large drink of water. I woke Kevin and he drove us back to the campsite. Everyone looked green but I was sort of fine. We met others from the other bus and six of them had been horribly sick all night.

Maybe because I don't normally drink or maybe I have the constitution of an ox, but I could have driven that bus back to Dover with no problem. Only I didn't know how to drive at the time, minor problem.

Well the best thing for a massive hangover is a mountain hike. That's where we headed. Neuschwanstein Castle. We parked at the base and, BLOODY HELL!!, it's a long hike up.

From the road below it doesn't look that daunting but it's an optical illusion. Trudge we did and the castle just kept getting further away. Halfway up there was a little Gnome type man yodelling his heart out. I'm sure he was put there to make you keep on trekking. I wanted to scone him. Not too keen on yodelling.

Anyway, finally made it and still had a little oxygen left in my blood steam so I took the tour of the castle. It's a fine thing, a bit over the top and glitzy but impressive. A reel or two of photos taken and down the mountain we go. That's a whole lot easier. Also, good fun telling the people coming up that they're nearly at the top when they actually have only just started the climb. Love being mean. Haha.

Next we headed back through Austria into Switzerland and landed in Liechtenstein. We got there about ten at night and yet again more rain. We parked the bus opposite a little English pub where everyone piled in. I didn't stay too long that night and crept back to the bus.

On the mountain is the palace which was all flood-lit. The night sky was so dark, the mountain seemed to have disappeared. It gave the illusion of a floating castle.

Back through Switzerland and we stopped this time in Lucerne. Perfect timing in a way because it was August 1st and that is Switzerland National day. Every shop was shut but the normally reserved people were in party mode and the evening sky was alive with fireworks.

Heidelberg was next on the agenda and the biggest wine barrel in the world took our attention. The beer hall served lager in giant glass boots which gets passed from person to person and isn't meant to be put down. I think the guys shared a couple of these before they went back to the usual manner of drinking. The girls took one look and decided that Munich was still too fresh in our memory to even attempt this latest challenge.

The Rhine river cruise sounded posh but again we were rained in so we could just about see a few castles in the mist but the apple strudel and hot chocolate on offer went down very well.

Nearing the end of our tour now and the gaping friendship divide slowly diminished as the magic of Europe engulfed us. I don't think the two groups will ever be bosom buddies but at least we can safely leave axes around and there won't be a fear of it being lodged in anyone's head anymore.

Amsterdam: Just had to hire a bike. I went about 17km and it was the easiest ride I'd ever had. Past windmills, flat ground, typical Dutch houses and a stop at a café for a taste of typical Dutch food. Whatever that was.

Back in time for the night crawl around the famous Red-Light District with women in shop windows wearing hardly anything and looking bored. The souvenir shops sold INTERESTING things and the guys were spruiked at constantly. One of them pulled the insides out of his trouser pockets to prove he had no money left.

Midnight we left that town and headed for Bruges. One last Party Piece from the bus though. We didn't make it to the campground, instead we ground to a stop with a flat tyre, so stayed just where we were for the night and it got fixed in daylight the next day.

A consolation though. We made it in good time for the ferry, but it still didn't make the overnight trip any more comfortable. They've had six weeks to put comfortable seating in but, no, they were still the same old uncomfortable ones we had at the start of this epic tour.

Back in England we said our goodbyes and gathered up all our dirty clothes and even dirtier sleeping bags and souvenirs. I boarded a train to Epsom and was so glad to see Gina waiting at the station for me.

## *Chapter 21*

# It Was Bound to Happen

## Unexpected

*Back view of the S.S. Britanis in Amsterdam*

My Australian visa

Was it ready?

Was it heck!

Australia House had the papers for seven weeks, but I was still told to come back tomorrow. They wanted to keep it, but I needed traveller's cheques, so they couldn't.

The Britanis was due into Tilbury on my birthday and I had two plans.

1. Travel with Yannis around Europe. Or

2. Re-join the ship. Which or whatever.

It was *roll the dice* time.

The day before the ship came in my passport got stamped. **Hoo Bloody Ray!!**

The night before the ship came in, I stayed with Vicky in Cheswick. It was a Britanis reunion because two of the nurses were also bunking up there for the night. We were going to converge en masse.

We always feel a little like celebrities when we turn up at the docks. The greetings are like meeting your fans, even though it's the wrong way around.

I found Yannis and he had the longest face. Oh well, plan number two. The Chief Purser said there was a vacancy for a stewardess, but I had to sign on at the London office. How fast can I travel? Lightning speed is the answer.

Tilbury docks to London Chandris office, sign on the dotted line. Zoom back to Epsom to pack, buy an airline ticket, caught a flight from Gatwick and met the ship in Amsterdam the very next day. Phew! Third time lucky.

This cruise will take us up to Scandinavia and Russia then on to the Mediterranean before finally docking in Greece. The crew have already done this run a couple of times so no big deal to them, but I've never been here before. It seems funny wearing a cardigan with the uniform and even though its summer a coat is needed whenever we went ashore.

In Gdansk, Poland I even saw people sunbathing on the beach. The older ladies did look like beached whales, I suppose all that extra blubber kept the chill out.

The rules were very strict here. We could only take the maximum of $20 and when the money is changed the bank slip is precious, never to be lost because it is checked on returning to the ship. If anyone is caught with Black Market money or goods, everything is confiscated, plus you get fined. Custom officials pace the decks peering into everything with their beady eyes.

My hours were from 8.30 am until 12.30 pm and then 6 pm until midnight so I got the whole afternoon off. The girls in the cabin seemed nice and as an added bonus the cabin is kept clean because some bright spark thought of making a roster.

I had a wonderful surprise a couple of days in. A tap on my shoulder, I turned around and who should be standing there? Nick from the Australis. Fantastic to see him, but O Oh, what about Yannis? Slightly tricky situation, but it had been a long while and people do move on.

Nick was now the Captain's personal steward which was quite a promotion but not much time off unfortunately. He seemed to accept the fact that we could now be just friends.

Forty-eight hours in Leningrad, Russia so I didn't go ashore the first day because I wasn't feeling all that bright. The next day the crew had a free tour of the Hermitage. All a bit rushed and then back in the bus as we drove past those beautiful golden domed buildings which I couldn't photograph as the bus was going too fast.

The passengers don't tip as freely or as generously as the American and Canadian passengers, but I didn't do too badly, I could still be as cheeky as I was renowned for.

Five days in I was struck down by the worst back and stomach pains that I can ever remember. The water was heavily chlorinated, and

I'd been drinking gallons of the stuff. I thought that was the problem. Then the vomiting started.

The ship's doctor was getting excited as he predicted appendicitis. The scalpels were being sharpened and he was swatting up on his "Anatomy Surgery for Beginners" books.

The nurses rescued the situation by putting a call in to the Captain and as soon as the ship docked in Stockholm I was whisked away to hospital.

The pain was so severe that I don't know if I arrived by ambulance or horse and cart. I was in and out of consciousness. Mountains of tests followed by truck loads of drugs. I stayed in an unconscious state for a while.

Once I woke up the nurse simply said "Moron". God, what had I turned into I fretted, grabbing the little mirror on the cabinet beside my bed? I didn't look any different from the pasty person I'd been for the last couple of days, not quite green any more just deathly white, but not a Moron surely. Later I found out this was just a greeting meaning "Good morning" She must have thought I was terribly vane.

My ailment wasn't my appendix after all. I had a nasty kidney infection called Pyelitis and I'd been putting up with the discomfort for too long rather than seeing medical help when the pain first started (actually when I was on the bus trip). Now it was a full-blown infection and in hospital I had to stay. Once before when I was ten years old the same thing happened, but even though I was put in hospital that time also, the pain wasn't as severe.

The ship had gone and left me. Yannis rang the hospital a couple of times and was relieved when I could actually talk to him.

By the Wednesday I was feeling back to my old self, but they wouldn't let me out until Sunday. My arms were empty of blood because of all the tests and I don't think they trusted me to see a doctor when I got back to England (they were right, I didn't).

The other ladies in my ward were lovely and they'd get their relatives to bring me sweets. One lady gave me her name and phone number and said if I was ever back in Sweden to call her and she would take me yachting on the lakes.

The porter came in with a television on a trolley all tangled up with aerials and cables and a grin from ear to ear. There was an English show and he thought I might like it. The show was **Fawlty Towers** and I'd never seen anything as mad since **Monty Python**. It was funny. My room mates wonder about not only my sanity, but the sanity of a whole nation of Brits. Couldn't blame them of course.

The journey back to England turned out to be an epic saga. I left the hospital with all my luggage at a quarter to three in the afternoon, took a taxi to the Stockholm shipping agent where they issued me with a plane ticket, grabbed another cab to the airport.

The plane was leaving soon, I had quite a way to go so the driver put on his racing helmet and zoomed in and out of the traffic flashing lights and beeping like a man possessed and he got me there with ten minutes to spare.

I raced in, presented myself to customs and they looked all over my passport but couldn't work out how I'd got into the country in the first place. No stamps, nothing. I hurriedly told them what happened. They dubiously let me board. Probably figured that I could be someone else's problem.

Had to change planes in Copenhagen with a one hour wait time. I didn't have any Danish money, so a lovely Hungarian man bought me an orange juice and we chatted until it was time to board. We sat in that plane for ages and ages. The door wouldn't shut apparently. Finally arriving at Heathrow at 9pm.

It was a bit late when I rang Gina and asked if I could come and stay. Talk about short notice!

Well I could for one night as they were off on holiday the next day.

All I heard was "Yes".

Finally, I managed to squeeze myself onto the third overpacked bus going to a London train station. I had no idea which station it was taking me to. Obviously looking distressed and knackered, my arms were full of puncture marks which my short-sleeved top didn't hide. (I must have looked like a junkie). When out of the gloom of desolation which was my mood, a knight in shining armour came to my rescue.

He gathered me and my suitcase up, found out my destination and took me not only to Victoria Station but stayed with me until my Epsom train arrived and helped me on the train with my suitcase.

He told me he was from Brazil; I don't remember his name and I don't know if I thanked him. I hope I did. I hope my good-mannered upbringing was in auto pilot.

*Chapter 22*

# Shhhhh...

## Don't Tell My Mother

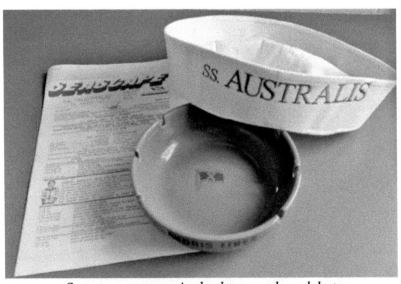

*Seascape ,a souvenired ashtray and a cob hat*

Poor Gina. She must have thought her home had a swinging door when it came to my multiple stopovers. I really couldn't stay this time though, so I rang Uncle Alan early the next morning. He and his partner had only just got back from holiday and Bill had returned to the Middle East where he worked, so Alan said there was room for me. I didn't know this uncle of mine all that much, but we got on like a house on fire.

The whole lounge room had strange dangly vines strung up all over the furniture. On these vines were oval shaped brown baubles. They turned out to be dates. Bill had brought them home and once they ripened up the flavour was irresistible.

Alan had a post lady who fancied him. Instead of the letters sliding through the letterbox in the door, she always had some reason to ring the bell and chat with him. Alan asked me to stay in my nightclothes and answer the door to her, which I did on a couple of occasions. She was very disappointed seeing me, but it did the trick and the mail was delivered in the usual way from then on.

When I was feeling back to my normal self again, Alan asked me to dress up in my sexiest outfit including high heels and come to the local pub with him.

Sure, why not. Any excuse to dress up and be taken out is good enough for me. But I am 172cm (5 foot 8 inches) tall in bare feet, when you add another 12cm (5 inches) for the high heels I towered over my tiny uncle who is a mere 154cm (about 5-foot 1 inch) tall. Add to this, him holding my hand and looking lovingly into my eyes. His friends were gob smacked to say the least.

Bill had only just left and here was Alan, canoodling up to the strange woman. His friends tried heavens hard to get me alone, but he just wouldn't let go of my hand. Finally, someone asked straight outright.

"Who are you?" I simply told the truth and said I was his niece from Australia. Everyone in the bar burst out laughing and didn't believe a word of it. Oh, did I mention it was a gay bar?

God that was a fun night.

Heading back into Cheswick a couple of days later I was relating my woes to Vicky. The Britanis would have finished the cruises by now, or nearly anyway. I had absolutely no idea what my next move would be. A group of the people sharing or bunking down at Vicky's flat were about to take off around the Mediterranean in a few days and a light bulb moment went off in my head.

This would need concise planning if it would work.

First, head to the Chandris office and ask if there was a ship heading for Melbourne. My luck was in. Could I work on the ship for a free passage home? The answer was in the affirmative. All I had to do was make my way down to Southampton and board. Yippee!!

Now the secret plan. I wrote four letters and put dates that I wanted them posted on the envelope where the stamp would be placed. I handed the letters to the guys who were taking off around the Med. And they promised to post them from which ever country they were in on the date I'd written.

I always wrote to mum and dad every week, so I needed this to work if I was to get away with my devious plan.

Every relative I could trust was sworn to secrecy as I bade them all farewell and thanked them from the bottom of my heart for looking after me when I was in most need, plus the fun I'd had reconnecting with them all.

The day arrived. I boarded the Australis again, not as a passenger this time but crew. It felt strange and sadness engulfed me. I wasn't ready to throw in the towel of world travel but the previous illness, no money, no place to lay my weary head and absolutely no idea what I could be doing lead me to this conclusion.

I didn't know any of the girls. Some were completely new to stewardessing and some were old hands at it. As usual we were thrown in at the deep end with a sink or swim attitude and off, we went. To my delight though, George the chief steward was on board and he recognized me. Ah, a friend. I told him of my strange work situation, and he promised to look after me.

This ship was full of either migrant families heading for the new world or returning freewheeling young travellers heading home with stories to delight their families for years to come. None, however had money to throw at stewardesses for tips so this would be a lean voyage for me. At least I had a bed to sleep in, clothes to wear and food to eat. The fun bit would come naturally.

SEASCAPE was the name of our daily newspaper printed on board with all the upcoming passenger events, sea temperatures, general information and upcoming ports of call. Plus, a quote of the day. The first day's quote was one of Oscar Wilde's favourites.

*"There is only one thing worse than being talked about – and that is not being talked about."*

Hmm, not so sure about that one.

The second night on board was the dreaded cocktail parties which had us all in a dither. On this voyage they had three sittings, so therefore three cocktail parties. Ahh!! Standing in military formation we stewards and stewardesses looking neat and confident with big beaming smiles ready to welcome the new arrivals. Three bloody times. Oh, so glad when they were all over. Was it a coincidence that the next quote for the day was:

*"To err is human, to forgive is divine"*

We were on our way to Heraklion in Crete, first port of call and change over for quite a few Greek crew. They were so excited; some hadn't seen family for months. This was also our first Time Change day. Always a bit of a laugh, someone usually forgets and has a rude awakening when they find out they are an hour late for work.

It never takes long for passengers to settle in and decide their favourite bar. The migrant families didn't look so lost and scared by about day three, more notices in the Seascape practically begging parents to rein in their wild children from fiddling with the safety equipment, especially the life rings.

We girls have now sorted out our shifts and as usual the chief steward finds it a whole lot easier if he allows friends to work the same hours even if we are in different bars.

I made a great friend called Rona. She was so bright, quick witted and funny. It wasn't long before George, the chief steward noticed that putting us together in the same bar could be catastrophic to say the least. We could find madness and mayhem in even the most ordinary circumstances.

Passengers noticed it too and loved it if either of us was on duty. The barmen were on edge because they thought they ruled but when we were together, they had no chance.

The funniest day came when as usual the Greeks were having a field day talking about us in their own language when all of a sudden Rona vented a tirade of verbal abuse all in Greek back to them. The look on their faces was a sight to behold. They didn't realize that she was a Cypriot from London. I never actually asked her what they had been saying or in fact what she said to them. Didn't need to know because the shocked look on their faces said it all.

As I said the tips were pretty lean on this voyage and completely non-existent when we had to take our turn for Bouillon or Afternoon Tea. Day after day people would try the Bouillon and decide they still didn't like it so trays full of overflowing cups had to be cleaned up.

Afternoon tea was worse. You would offer lemon or milk, some wanted both. No matter how hard you tried to explain that that simply doesn't work, they would get really adamant that this is what they liked and wanted, so when the tea was poured, milk added and then in went the slice of lemon my wicked sense of humour enjoyed watching them try and drink the horrible curdling mess. I liked to hang around for a while to watch them enjoying" themselves. Later, more cleaning up of curdled scummy cups. '

After Heraklion we headed for Port Said and the passengers who could afford it had an early morning start for a bus trip into Cairo. I of course had to work and couldn't go but a group of us did go ashore in Port Said and I'm glad some of the male crew came as well.

Practically straight away greasy little men would slide up to the guys and offer 'Dirty postcards' we had a look and they were so tame. The guys just refused. Then they were offered 'Spanish Fly', very intriguing. The hand gestures and innuendo towards we females was quite offensive but I did find it all hilariously funny.

It was just like being in an old black and white movie film. *"Hey, Mister! You wanna buy my seester?"*

In nine days, we had five time changes. It got to the stage where I was getting up before I even went to bed. The days were warm and sunny so snoozing in the afternoon on deck was heavenly except for the dreaded sun burn. Luckily by now I was an old hand at dodging those nasty rays and knew just how much I could take. A lot of passengers were lured into thinking that as it wasn't that hot, they would be spared the inconvenience of sun burn even though they were warned daily to slap on the sunscreen and protect their children's heads. The reflective rays from the sea are deadly.

I wonder who chose the Quotes for the day on the Seascapes. Some are so appropriate to the way I'd been feeling and some just made me laugh out loud.

For example – Good Morning – *Kalimera.*

That was always written but on one day it was followed with, *"To generalise is to be an idiot."*

Did they mean the *Good* part of the *Morning*?

We were in Djibouti that day and 'Good' wasn't the word I would have chosen for that port. It was dirty and dusty. A place for lost souls. We weren't there long, maybe I was being too harsh, still as they say; First Impressions.

I hoped the guys were posting my letters home. By now they should have sent two. I was missing words from home. Mum wrote to me every week and I did the same. She probably thought I was having a fabulous time soaking up the Mediterranean elegance rather than working my heart out serving drinks and carting sandwiches around. This was so different from cruising.

The entertainment staff were hard at it constantly finding fun and exciting things for passengers of all different age groups to be kept joyful. Food was varied daily and even where people could choose to eat was taken into consideration. Often there would be a buffet lunch on the promenade deck rather than having to go down to the dining room if you didn't want to.

There were keep Fit Classes, Charm school (don't know if anyone went to those) deck games, library, board games and totes on the ship's run. Plenty of time for love affairs but nowhere to hide if it failed. All in all, being on a voyage has nothing in comparison to real life.

By the time we reached Fremantle everyone had partaken in fancy dress, vice-versa night, pub quizzes, discos, cabaret shows, two more cocktail parties and met up with the King himself. No not Elvis but Neptune. I had a ball. The passengers were so much fun and were up to being teased and tormented as much as they did it to Rona and I.

All people disembarking in Australia had to undergo a medical examination. Like all the passengers I also had to undergo this. It wasn't much and I was issued with my pink slip. I didn't actually ask what happens to people who don't pass the examination. Did they get tossed overboard before we reached Fremantle I wondered?

About five of us girls went ashore together in Fremantle and our legs wobbled and shook being on hard ground again. It is such a strange sensation. We'd heard that Aussie pubs didn't really except females so that's where we headed first. It was the most blokey pub we could find. We all rocked up to the bar and ordered beers. The barman looked worried as he served us. The guys hanging onto the counter stared and grumbled so we hung on to the counter as well. We only had one drink, but we'd made our point and did a much more interesting thing. Went shopping.

Back on board we had a change of currency. Instead of Pounds Sterling we were now using Australian dollars. I hadn't seen these for a couple of years, but it didn't take long to get used to them again. Unfortunately not all the passengers were that happy with the changeover and a lot of discussions were had with the barmen. Grumbles in other words.

The sea was also getting rougher. It had been so warm and calm but now we were heading for the Great Australian Bight and it's notorious for rolling seas. Ropes had to be put up between lounges and door kept shut. People who thought they were good sailors suddenly realized that their stomachs didn't agree.

Rona was grabbing in mid-air for the ropes as we carried trays of drinks from one bar to another. I thought she was doing her usual mucking about and found this whole charade extremely funny until I found out that she was actually blind in one eye and had no field of distance, the fumbling was for real. I still found it extremely funny.

The lounge bar towards the front of the ship had a fairground view of the waves. We would pitch upwards into the sky and then crash down into the sea. Only the few hardy brave souls remained. A group of young guys were ordering beers like they were going out of fashion and kept Rona and I busily stumbling about getting them. Finally, they asked for sick bags. I told them to bugger off as I had a weak stomach, which they did. BUT they left a full sick bag on the table and I had to take it away. YUK! I picked it up very carefully and started going green myself when I heard them all laughing from the doorway. They'd just filled the bag up with beer to see my reaction.

Melbourne arrived and I became the same as a disembarking passenger. The hugs and the tears all came flooding over me. I was excited to be going home but at the same time I didn't want this madness to end. Gathering up my suitcase and heading for customs I waved to my friends a final farewell.

The Seascape quote was:

*"It is never good dwelling on goodbyes, it is not the being together that it prolongs, it is the parting."*

Carrying my suitcase and a large tin of Quality Street toffees I walked off Station Pier and started down Beaconsfield Parade. I stuck my thumb out and within a couple of minutes a Combi van pulled over and asked where I was heading.

"Frankston, I said, so he said "Hop in."

It took about an hour and, on the way, I told him of my intended surprise to my family. Thank goodness he wasn't a mass murderer because nobody knew I was coming home, and nobody knew him.

Instead he took me all the way to the street at the back of my house where I waved goodbye, threw my suitcase and sweets over the fence and then climbed up and landed in the chicken run. Snuck my way through Dad's vegetable garden and then burst in through the back door and yelled

**"Hello"**.

......Nothing.

Mum and Dad had visitors and Dad was in the kitchen making tea... Everybody was stunned silent and just stared. Not a word was spoken. I held up the Quality Street and said,

"Well if I give you these will you let me in?"

and at the same time, I touched Dad on the shoulder. He let out a huge sigh of relief and said

"She's alive!" ...What??

Dad who was a complete and utter atheist thought I'd died and come back to say goodbye. He thought he was the only one who could see me. It was only when I touched him, he realized I was real.

Well that wasn't the greeting I was expecting! Mum picked up a clipping from the newspaper and showed it to me. It was the arrival time of the Australis. She said she had a feeling. Hmm, did those guys post my letters home I wondered?

*Chapter 23*

# Can't See the Wood
## for the Trees

*Trees in an Australian forest*

OK so I'm home.

Great to see Mum, Dad, my dog Nipper, new addition to the family, Rory a boxer dog who's both previous people had died, Snowy & Gungadhin the pussy cats, Heidi & Genevieve the goats, all the chickens and my brother Robert."

**BUT!**

What am I doing here? Of course, I went back to the supermarket and got a job in the deli. Caught up with friends. Some had got married; one was even having a baby.

*OH MY GOD*!!! Noooooo!

There was a Chandris office in Melbourne. Could they, would they let me back on again? Only one way to find out and that was to front up to Chandris House in Collins Street and ask.

As luck would have it the Australis was due back and ...

**Christmas Carnival Cruise** was scheduled to leave Melbourne on the 18th December 1976. It was only for nineteen days around the South Pacific gathering up more people in Sydney and Auckland.

Yes, I could sign up, but I had to sign up for two of these cruises and not disembark until the 25th January 1977.

Mum and Dad were dubious. This felt like a rerun of what happened in England. They wanted me to settle down but how could I with so much more of the world to see. I told them this was only for just over a month then I'd be home again.

*Chapter 24*

# Christmas Carnival Cruises

## I'm Back

**L-R**: *Fiona (the DJ), 3 passengers, me, a passenger & Jean*

The staff captain told me he'd missed me and had to cry himself to sleep every night.

George the Chief Steward still wanted to rape me and tried to lock me in a cupboard. The passengers got a laugh every time I called him a dirty old man.

Nick was back working up in the bars like me and it was great to see him again. The ship felt the same and everyone was pleased to see me. Even my mad mate Rona was still onboard.

These cruises feel so much different than the voyages. I'm sure the entertainment crew found these few weeks a welcome change. A respite from recruiting amateurs, now they could strut their stuff and show everyone what they were really made of.

I couldn't believe my luck when shown to my two-berth cabin. At first it was going to be shared with a dining room waitress who had completely different working hours so a quick shuffle around and Jean, another stewardess became my cabin mate. We both work in the bars and finish quite late so don't have to worry about disturbing each other. I was hoping to share with Rona but as Jean and I had been hired specifically for these two cruises we'd been given special accommodation.

The working day is usually ten hours broken into a couple of shifts. Mine started at 2pm and finished about 1am with time off for dinner. The new girls find it challenging but I was expecting that even though Chandris House told me I'd be working an eight-hour day. There are also Chandris inspectors on board, so everyone is on their best behaviour.

We went to Sydney, Auckland, Suva, Lautoka, Santo, Vila, and Noumea then back to Melbourne on the first cruise. Christmas day was at sea and even two days before there seemed to be no word of any parties.

New Year's Eve had a completely different atmosphere. We were all up in the main lounge ready to dish out the mega volumes of free champers. Passengers were also ordering their own better quality bottles and I became quite adept at opening these at speed.

Rona and I became quite competitive with who could pop a cork quickest. We aimed for light fittings, each other's legs, any officers who crossed our paths we even tried duelling. Who needs professional entertainment when we worked together?

Unfortunately, the fridges weren't keeping up with the cold bottles and by midnight they were beginning to feel a little on the warm side. I was hovering over some glasses with a fresh bottle of bubbly in my hands ready for the opening when the countdown started. The lights went out; POP! Goes the champagne and bubbles gush everywhere. I shove the neck of the bottle into my mouth to stop the overflow and gulp as quickly as I could. When the light came back on nobody was the wiser as I professionally poured into each glass. Rona guessed what I had just done because the tell-tale signs of champagne dribbling down my chin gave me away.

## Happy New Year. 1977

I don't know if anyone remembers going to Noumea on the 1st of January. It's a bit of a dodgy memory for me that's for sure.

Cruise A19A finishes and cruise A20A starts. Here we go again. This time we've got a couple of different ports to call into. One is Tonga another is Apia.

Jean and I were worked down in the disco for some of our shifts on the last cruise. Now they want us to be there permanently. I had a feeling the top brass were separating Rona and I. The little lounge had all been rigged up with new furniture and carpets and they are calling it the Night Club area. Fiona the DJ was doing her best to drum up more punters by having theme nights, but it was still a little too quiet. It was actually a bit boring.

All the stewardesses were called up to the Captain's quarters for a pep talk. George, the chief steward, The Chief Purser and the Staff Captain were also there so it was a bit crowded. I was sitting on the floor in front of George and whilst the Captain was droning on and on. I was plucking the hairs out of George's legs. He couldn't show any pain or flinch, but I'd get a sharp knee in my back when no one was looking. I wonder what the Captain was talking about for all that time?

Eventually the disco became a hive for the younger teens and sometimes it was really crowded. They were all good fun kids, too old for children's entertainment but too young for adult stuff, obviously their parents were happy they had a place to go. We'd created a special space out of the critical sight of the top officers and parents.

Sometimes Fiona the DJ had to be in another entertainment area, so I became Disco Queen. It was great fun and we'd celebrate everybody's birthday. It was cheating really because everyone got to choose what song they wanted me to play.

Going ashore in Samoa a group of us came upon a little village where everyone was in a state of great excitement. We had unexpectedly stumbled into a native Samoan wedding and were instantly invited to join the party. We were led to a long hut with no walls just a grass pitched roof, told to sit on the woven mats, given banana leaves plates and served all sorts of food. The shade was a welcome relief from the hot sun. I ate the vegetable things and passed the meat over. Luckily nobody took offence to this.

I couldn't help noticing how hugely fat some of the people were. Later I found out that it is a status symbol to be that massive. Especially for the chief. Heart attack material more likely though.

One night the weather was a bit rough. A cyclone was on its way which meant we had to deviate away from Tonga. We had an extra day in Suva. It was amazing seeing great tall palm trees bending right over in the wind and that wasn't even the main cyclone. A lot of the passengers were scared and stayed in their cabins. The ropes were up, and Rona and I thought it would be a real laugh if we walked around with our life jackets on. Although George saw the funny side, he recommended that we didn't do that or we'd be fined, plus someone might have a heart attack. Kill Joy!!

Still we did have some excitement. During Bingo a man had a fit, his eyes rolled back in his head, his body went stiff and then he shit himself. YUK. Rona managed to take out his false teeth whilst I rang the hospital. (I'm glad it was that way around). The nurse came up instantly and took charge and then he was carried off to the hospital on a stretcher.

This final cruise was coming to an end and I was dreading going back home. I asked if I could stay on. The answer was yes, but I'd have to go back to Southampton as a free passage. In other words, work but no pay. What to do? George said he'd fix up my pay sheet and make it look like I did more hours to get an overtime rate for these two cruises. I ended up with about four hundred British Pounds. This was going to have to last me until I got my next paying job, whatever and wherever that would be.

On January 25th, 1977 I waved goodbye to Mum and Dad again and said I'd see them in two months.

Did I see them again in two months? The answer is no. Instead George my boss found out that the Britanis was going to be in Curacao a few days after we docked. They needed extra staff. A cashier, a photographer and an engineer. Would I like to be that cashier? Would I ever!! And I'd be getting paid.

Going through the Panama Canal again George, Jean, Fiona and I decided to have our own farewell party in a hamburger joint in Balboa. Not the classiest of places but we had fun.

The next day the chief purser wanted to see me. He asked why I wanted to leave. My honest answer was money. I would be getting paid on the Britanis and I had no idea what was around the corner for me once I got back to England. He kindly said that I was his best stewardess and asked George to find someone else, but that may have just been kind words, which I very much appreciated.

My last day on board became a free day. I had my hair streaked blonde and it looked great. A champagne party was organized for the early hours of the morning when all my friends had finished work. The day was mine to wander. One of the passengers came up and asked me to go to the disco with him and have my photo taken. When I got there about twenty of the kids had a signed card and presented me with a giant furry toy rabbit. A teary moment.

Later back in my cabin I heard a knock on the door and the

steward said the Captain wanted to see me. He had written me a beautiful reference all in English because he knew I'd want to know what he said. How true was that!! He gave me a kiss on the head and also gave me the line of being the best stewardess. I can take as much praise as anyone wants to give me, whether it's blather or not.

My party that night was brilliant and finished about 6.30 in the morning.

In Curacao, Rod the Master at Arms took me ashore for our own goodbyes. I'd been seeing him for the last few weeks and even though nothing was ever going to be permanent or heavy, we were still pretty good friends. All these special goodbyes were beginning to get to me.

I had to be back on board by midday when the agent was coming to collect Sinclair, the photographer, Spiro the engineer and me and take us to a hotel where we were to spend the next four days with the compliments of Chandris whilst we waited for the Britanis to arrive.

Quickly I scribbled a letter home telling them my good news with a promise of a new mailing list as soon as I knew it. Now all I wanted was for my friend Rona to come along but unfortunately that didn't happen, and I've never seen her again.

Our letters crossed and missed each other, and I know she got married and her surname changed as did mine and she has been lost to me ever since. Such a shame, we had so much fun and I'm sure there's still a lot of mischief that we could conjure up if ever we were to meet again.

## Chapter 25
# An Island in the Sun
## Curacao

*Old man with his donkey in Curacao with Spiro and I*

Who would have thought it? An actual paid holiday on a Caribbean Island, with two men to look after me as well.

The Britanis wasn't due into Curacao until Saturday. It was the same schedule for cruising as last year so that meant we had four whole days of complete freedom all at the expense of Mr. Chandris. Well, not totally at his expense. We did pitch in and hire a car so we could get further around than our hotel rooms. We each had our own room by the way and even though they weren't the most luxurious, they were clean and comfortable with the added bonus of giant beautifully coloured lizards that would scuttle in if the door was left open.

Curacao is quite a baron island as it's one of the first to get hit by the annual cyclones in this area. The landscape is rugged and just to add to the inhospitably it grows massive cacti sprouting lethal red pointy spikes. From a distance it looks like red grass with Wild West type cactus on the hillsides, but it's just a rouse, the spiky red grass are baby cacti ready to impale you.

Sinclair was inspired by this and had a double barrel camera rigged up and took copious amounts of photos. He even got me modelling in some ridiculous situations. How to look sexy and demure when at even the slightest slip I could have been punctured by the local flora or washed out to sea as a rogue wave drags me from the confines of a sea cave. It was great being around an artist though because it made me take notice of things that I could easily have missed.

We found old abandoned Dutch looking houses which we trespassed into. Grottos on the shore that the sea had eaten into, trees that were blown nearly over but still hung on and then along the road an old man and his donkey which was laden down with sugar cane.

We asked if we could have a photo with him and he was a bit unsure, especially as Spiro grabbed his huge cane cutting knife and posed with it like he was going to cut off the poor bloke's head. Sinclair quickly shot a few snaps and we thanked the old man whilst Spiro returned the knife to its rightful place.

We told Spiro how stupid had been to do that, but he just became all Greek and didn't understand our tirade.

## Chapter 26
# Just Like A Bad Penny
## Life Mapped Out

*Old map of the West Indies*

I wonder how many times you can keep turning up before you wear out your welcome?

This was actually going through my mind as I fronted up to the purser's deck yet again.

To my delight I was embraced back into the bosom of the ship's community.

Obviously once a Chandris girl, always a Chandris girl. Many kisses and hugs from officers, barmen and stewards, maybe a tad over enthusiastically. Eventually released from their embraces and shown to my cabin which was on A Deck this time.

I met with the two girls I was to share a four-berth cabin with. We were all cashiers and now my uniform consisted of a blue coloured skirt instead of maroon. No more cleaning horrible smelly ashtrays. It also meant that I didn't get any tips but at least I was going to be paid, eventually.

Sinclair settled in quickly and liked the two photographers that he worked with. We took each other to the beach in St Thomas and swapped stories. Spiro took a little longer to settle but eventually got into the rhythm of a new ship and its surroundings. I didn't see much of him after the first couple of days, different areas and work schedules and all that sort of thing.

The first bar I worked in was The Gallery. To my surprise Nick, my Nick from Australis passenger days was the barman. It was wonderful to see him again. There weren't as many cashiers as stewardesses and we got moved around quite a lot which I didn't mind. The work for a cashier is very, very easy compared to a stewardess but the hours are quite long, and I worried that my bum was going to spread like uncooked bread dough with all the sitting.

That meant late night runs around the deck just to try and keep my hourglass figure. This could be dangerous as that's when the night shift deck hands hose everything, it becomes like an ice rink and if the sea decides to give a little rock and roll anything could happen. Obviously, my core strength was in tip top condition and I never fell overboard.

The Britanis needed a cashier because they lost one. Not overboard running around the deck at night but sent home for family reasons. I don't know why they needed an extra photographer and engineer; maybe the previous ones had taken an unexpected dip?

A few weeks into my new role, Wendy, another cashier had a tragic phone call from home saying that her father had died suddenly. The poor girl collapsed. Her father hadn't even been ill. It was so unexpected and took days to get a flight organized.

Chandris were wonderful and did the very best to help get her home safely. But now with Wendy gone our working hours increased sometimes up to fourteen hours a day or even more.

That's when I changed my mind about Cocktail parties. They were no longer my worst nightmare especially if by some freak coincidence I was fortunate enough to be rostered in the Marine bar. On those occasions that bar was closed so the barmen could organize the free booze and I could slink off for a few hours.

We had a bit of trouble in the one of the bars for a while. It seemed that the cash register lost its ability to add up properly; funny how it was never over but always short. This didn't look good for me or any of the other girls. Nobody actually blamed anyone. I needed a devious plan to swart my accusers. With secret marks I scribbled on the paper till roll whenever I vacated my chair for dinner breaks then I could prove my innocence. Thank god that worked and miraculously the cash register improved its mathematical skills.

Peter was a cute little barman and stood at the great height of five feet tall if he pulled his shoulders back, stomach in and stood on a box. He wasn't a push over by any means, in fact he could be just as grumpy as the rest, but he was still cute.

One Saturday we both had the time off and with a hired car, bathers and beach towels we headed for the beach. The one he found wasn't all that pretty and quite isolated. We soon found out why it wasn't on the top ten tourist favourite beauty spot list.

It was full of stones and rocks, no comfortable sand to sit on and lurking in the shallows, I obviously hadn't noticed, were sea urchins littering the sea floor which I managed to step on. Yeeouch!

If Peter had any devious thoughts about getting me alone, or romantic ideas, these prickly little critters put paid to that. I think I taught him a few new words in the English language that day and they were not very ladylike either.

Hobbling back to the car where I spent the next hour or more plucking spines out of my foot. The other barmen were giving Peter the old 'Wink, Wink, Nudge, Nudge look when we arrived back on board together. "What the hell did they think we had been up to?" I could hardly walk!

There were people that I knew from last time around, a few from the casino and of course stewards and barmen. It never took too long to meet the rest of the gang. The days ashore with the different mix of crew were always fun (except for the sea urchin episode). I'd go ashore with whoever was free on that day or had the same hours as me. We'd head to the beach, go shopping, sometimes sightseeing, the casino anything that seemed new and interesting.

Whilst sunbathing on the beach in Barbados one day, I looked up and saw a Yeti coming towards me. As it got closer, the hairy beast resembled someone I knew. It was actually the crew purser. Amazing what a beautifully pressed white uniform can hide. This guy had his own insulation. Nice guy though and from the neck up he's very attractive. I suppose I shouldn't say he's not without his clothes on though; you'll get the wrong impression.

The English or should I say, non-Greek crew had a favourite hangout in Curacao. It was nothing special, just an outdoor café that served beer and hotdogs. It became our meeting place which was renamed The Heineken Festival. Guaranteed someone would be there holding the fort or at least a beer. Passengers would ask us why the crew always ate ashore; didn't we have good food like they did? Well we actually had the same menu as the passengers up in the Officer's Mess, but it was so repetitive. Every week we had the same thing. We were craving junk food like hamburgers or hotdogs. Humans are never satisfied.

Back on-board Brian the DJ would play Midday Melodies for quiet reflecting times. He would sometimes ask if anyone had a request which wasn't always such a good idea. I'd ask for Rod Stewart, one barman asked for Daddy Cool and the other liked Barry White. Passengers would soon get in on the act and our quiet little relaxing siesta time seemed more like battle of the bands. Brian preferred that anyway, he liked being a disco DJ. Midday Melodies cramped his *Cool* style.

Crew parties are the same on all ships. Any excuse to have one will do. They always turned out to be loud, drunken and quite often, shall we say, indiscrete?

We had an English Master at Arms and he could be a very funny drunk and the best organizer of secret crew parties if he found an uninhabited cabin. They were always great fun and very squashy. It was hard keeping the noise down and sometimes there would be complaints. That's when we'd have to move off to the open decks. If we dressed in our civvies, we hoped passengers and other officers wouldn't realize we were crew. Don't think it fooled ANYONE.

Passengers make a real difference to your working week on cruises. Sometimes you can have a real laugh with them; other times they treat you like you're a servant. Again, we had the hordes of Venezuelans on like the previous year. Only the agents had overbooked and for two nights people were sleeping in the main lounges and even using the hospital beds.

The stewards and stewardesses were run off their feet and it wasn't a happy place. I had a relatively quiet time because they never buy drinks. Barmen are not Happy Chappies when they came aboard.

Twice I experienced Ash Wednesday on Martinique. It is actually scary. The day is dedicated to the **Joyeuses Pleureuses** '(devilettes, devils that cry for the death of Vaval), all dressed in black and white, the men are covered in sugar syrup and charcoal mourning for the death of Vaval, who is symbolically burnt on a bonfire at nightfall. The islanders have celebrated for weeks and each day they wear different costumes each steeped in tradition and superstition by the time they get to Ash Wednesday the mood can turn violent.

At the celebration's end the island enters the period of Lent, that leads up to Easter. Lent, the period of fasting and abstinence coincides with the dry season on Martinique. Tradition requires that one does not dance, listen to music and all weddings and other celebrations are postponed until afterwards.

Easter is Carnival time. The other islands seem to be more joyous. Parades, floats brightly coloured costumes and steel drumming. School children parade down the main street. It gets a bit frantic but fabulous to watch.

Add to that the Greek Orthodox Easter was the same week as everyone else's in 1977 so Parties every night!

Around the same time in San Juan a whole group of local kids would come aboard. The DJ would play Latin music for them in the disco. It wasn't really allowed but everyone turned a blind eye and the kids had a great time. The dancing is fabulous to watch, they have magic rhythm.

A little Latino guy who probably forgot to get off in time became an accidental stowaway. He was discovered looking very perplexed, anxious and alone by passengers who took him under their wing. This was a Caribbean cruise he would never have dreamt of. Well looked after, fabulous food and a comfortable bed all provided by a wonderfully sweet couple. When he arrived home a week later it was the hot topic for the local TV station.

The next week a couple of passengers couldn't get into their cabin and had to get the purser with a master key to open the door. Inside were three boys between the ages of ten to fourteen stowing away. The Staff Captain was called. He gave them a right telling off and said they'd be flown home the next day.

St Thomas was our next port and they were in the purser's office whilst flights were being arranged when they bolted. The ship was held up for over an hour and they just couldn't be found. They were ashore with only the clothes they were wearing, now far from home with no money or anything. We all hoped the police found them and sent them home. We never did find out.

Another unintentional stowaway happened to be a fully-grown man who should have known better. Basically, he was a chatterbox and either ignored the final chuck out announcements or thought he still had plenty of time until he felt the ship move. He was yelling to anyone who would listen that he wanted the ship to turn around and take him back to San Juan.

Peter the barman sent him to the Bridge and told him to ask the Captain. He marched up there all sure of himself and demanded the ship return to port. The Captain said he'd put him in the jail and he nearly shit himself (The captain is a stirrer). In the end he got himself so drunk that he slept the night on a lounge chair and flew home the next day.

Towards the end of the cruise season we were out at sea, a couple of sailors were getting petrol that was stored in a lifeboat when they discovered a young boy. They had a struggle to get him out of the boat as he put up quite a fight. Once they had him the sailor tossed him over his shoulder like a fireman's hold. The poor kid thought he was going to be thrown overboard and passed out. He was taken to the hospital and looked after by the nurses and when they found out his home island, he was able to stay on until we went back there. So lucky it wasn't our final port, or he would have gone all the way to Europe with us.

On this group of cruises, I didn't have a rich homosexual admirer who bought me many expensive gifts, instead I did have one very sweet Venezuelan boy who followed me around everywhere and tried to teach me Spanish. We swapped some coins. I gave him some Australian and he gave me some Venezuelan. I think he was a bit of a loner and as I just sit at my cash register, I'm easy pickings. When his weeks cruise was up, he gave me a bead necklace and a kiss.

While I was busy swapping ships a few months earlier, the Chandris office in Melbourne rang my home and offered me a job on the Ellinis. What a shame I missed that one. It was going around the South Pacific then up to Singapore, Japan and Hong Kong. All new places I hadn't seen. Also Rod who was Master at Arms on the Australis wrote to me and said he'd swapped and was now on the Ellinis. He said the ship was full of fifty-year olds so it would have been a quiet cruise.

When you're in your early twenties, a fifty-year-old is ancient. Little did we realize that when we got to that grand old age the world still rocked and rolled just as crazily and we hung on tight.

The Caribbean cruises finished for the year. The tugboats again shot water cannons into the sky. The deep whistles and horns from the Britanis in answer saying farewell as the steel drums on shore faded into the distance. This time we didn't call in to New York but headed straight for Europe. The passage over wasn't too bumpy but sitting by the open doors in the Marine bar brought out the goose pimples.

Madeira was our first port of call and even though it was springtime we all felt the chill.

My friend Charmaine and I went ashore with a group of waiters and we ended up in a street bar. The wine was local and quite delicious. Jean- Marie was a wine waiter and decided to buy some of the local stuff to take back to his home in the south of France. He left the ship in Vigo, Spain, which was a shame because he really was good fun. I had drunk too much, which isn't hard for me to do and it took a couple of hours for me to get my brain working properly again.

Next port was Lisbon and although I'd been there before it's always great to see a place with someone who's never been. Again, it was Charmaine. We were wandering aimlessly around when a fellow came up and asked if we needed any help. We asked the way into town and he gave us a lift. Then we did what most girls do in these situations, went shopping.

Warm clothes were needed as I had decided to stay onboard for at least one North Cape cruise. Last time was disastrous, I really wanted to see this part of the world.

When we next arrived in Vigo, it was time to say goodbye to Jean-Marie. I'd really only just met him. He was a wine waiter down in the dining rooms and our paths hadn't met until the previous port. He was happily heading home with many tales to tell no doubt.

I decided to walk into town following the tram tracks. The temperature was still a bit chilly but as town was further than I thought the exercise warmed me up. Grabbed a taxi ride back afterwards though.

Amsterdam saw us fare-welling a lot of the crew. Old off, new on. I was one of the three old cashiers who stayed on and two new girls joined. Even the Staff Captain from the Australis has joined the Britanis.

He will eventually take the reins but at the moment he's just learning all the routes. He's a lovely man the Britanis is lucky to have him.

While all this was going on Val, my cabin buddy, and I took in the sights of old Amsterdam including a river boat tour. We actually laughed about that. We'd been on a ship for months and then take to the water again. Slightly different though.

Stephanos, my boss had been fiddling with our work schedule which really didn't give anyone enough time to get ashore and have a good look around, so once again we took matters into our own hands and did it properly. Did he think we were on there just to work or something?

The further north we headed the colder it got. I was very wary of catching a chill and rugged up warmly. Going from thirty degrees to seven degrees in a matter of a couple of weeks shocks the system.

The ship moved slowly through the Kiel Canal in West Germany and the fields and little cottages on either side are so pretty. Even though I was at work the passing scenery was glorious. The pleasures of sitting at a bar with windows.

This time I got to see Stockholm. It's very pretty and walking through the parks there were so many people sunbathing, Brrrr. I still felt the cold. Leaving Stockholm, we cruised through the Fiords and saw mansions, cottages and wonderful forests. I bet it's spectacular in the winter all covered in snow.

The sun doesn't actually set it just gets a bit darker. The horizon had a glow of green and red and the clouds looked like little black sheep. The sea was calm with just a hint of white crested waves.

I went ashore early in Helsinki but couldn't even buy a postcard because they wouldn't take American money and I didn't want to change because they wouldn't change it back if I didn't spend it all. Instead I wandered for a couple of hours until I felt frozen enough and then went back on the ship for a long thawing out shower.

Leningrad was next. This was the first time I'd seen my passport for months. In every other place we'd been crew just wandered off and no questions asked. Not Russia though. We had our passports checked and checked again. Ushered onto a bus for the crew's free two-hour tour but as it was all in German, we had no idea what they were saying. Instead, Bernard, my French cousin as I called him decided to interpret. Mind you, he can't speak German either, but he made up a story from words that sounded vaguely French or English. It was hilarious and our tour guide was NOT impressed.

Some of the commentary was in English and it was all about how great the education system is and by the time a child reaches the grand old age of four, they already know what occupation it will have and that's where their schooling aims. No choice. I probably would have been prime Siberian Mine fodder.

They did actually stop the bus for us to take photos occasionally but whizzed past places we were not meant to see. Everyone seemed to be dressed in drab clothes and all were very pale. There were women and men doing roads works but mainly leaning on shovels. They get paid the same whether the work gets done or not apparently.

This made being in the bus as jolty as riding a horse, we bumped our way along on the pot holed road with some craters big enough to swallow a truck. Buildings still had scars from the Second World War with broken windows and fallen walls. Hundreds of soldiers and police were about all with red stripes somewhere on their uniforms also many, many red flags flying.

The tour ended and we were taken back to the ship. On no account were we or anyone else allowed to take photos from the deck. I saw one passenger ignore the warnings and within a matter of minutes he was accosted by Russian security guards. They were going to confiscate his camera.

He managed to beg and got it back but not the film. That had been ripped out. The problem for this guy was his film included shots of all the previous ports of call which were now lost. He had been warned like the rest of us. It was still a shame though.

In the evening the two new barmen, George and Theo and I were taken to the Seaman's club. We thought that would be rather boring but when we started to examine what was on offer we found a large library with books written in English mainly telling us the virtues of communism, chess boards all set up ready for a challenging game, I lost against George.

In the auditorium and lady and gentleman formally introduced a concert after telling us about 'The spring of happiness and peace they have found in their lives'. Then the singing started. Groan! The next act was a mime and he was fantastic. I think he was miming 'HELP!' Get me outta here, but I couldn't be certain.

The comedy act sent us scuttling to the bar. Soon it was time for me to head back to work. Unfortunately, I'd just missed the bus so paid a guy with a van a couple of beers and off we went.

Bloody hell, he was Russia's worst driver. He managed to find every pothole, disregarded any road signs, couldn't make up his mind which side of the road he preferred and played chicken with passing pedestrians. Amazingly no wheels fell off and I live to tell the tale. I don't know whether he was machismo or mental. Definitely a maniac.

The next afternoon was quiet and I asked if I could join the group going to the Summer Palace. This place is a copy of Versailles in France but of course they have their own story. Didn't matter anyway, it is beautiful.

I hoped that Bernard would be on the same tour because his interpretation is so much funnier. I was in luck. Wish I'd met him months ago. I didn't know such dishy French guys worked as wine waiters down in the dining rooms. Just my luck to find this out when I'd already decided to leave at the end of this cruise.

The new barmen that joined the ship in Amsterdam were great fun and didn't want me to be leaving. They kept giving me chocolates and making special cocktails tempting me to stay on until October but that felt like months away. Hang on! It was months away. I had no real idea of what was next in store for me, but I knew it wasn't staying on the ship. I'd had a taste of Europe and now I wanted more.

After Russia we headed to Gdynia. I again had the morning off so Val, George an electrician whose name has been lost in time to me and I jumped into a taxi, changed our money with the driver because the

Black Market had a better rate of exchange than a bank on the ship and headed into town.

What the driver didn't tell us though, was the shops were all shut on a Sunday. All this money and nothing to spend it on, except a taxi ride that is. He very kindly dropped us right outside a whore house where we noticed quite a few male crew members were considering the patronage of the personnel.

Oh well, not wanting to join the queue and not sure what to do with ourselves we headed for a pub. They were as behind the times as Fremantle where girls weren't allowed in so Val and I pretended to be blokes. That didn't work at all so off to a café.

We'd settle for a coffee and a sandwich. "What was a sandwich?" Everyone knows what coffee is but even our best charades and miming didn't get us any closer to a lump of cheese plonked between two pieces of bread. We had a bowl of soup.

Next stop Copenhagen. It was lovely arriving at six in the evening especially as I finished work at seven. It was light enough to enjoy views of the harbour and didn't get too dark.

The shop boys and a crowd of us girls headed for the Tivoli Gardens. One of the largest amusement parks in the world being more than eighty thousand square meters practically right in the heart of the city, it's truly magical.

The musical military band marched. We joined in before having a ride on the old Merry Go Round then the wooden roller coaster. There were so many fairy lights dressing the avenues of trees, light sculpture swans wearing crowns on a large man-made lake in this fantasy land.

It was a shame most of the girls had to start work at ten but as Val, the shop boys and I didn't have to start until eleven, we all strolled back together. Even though we didn't finish work until the wee small hours of the morning, Val and I managed to rouse ourselves and go ashore again early the next morning.

The sun was bright but still chilly. We felt sorry for the Little Mermaid sitting naked on a rock at the water's edge. She is a lot smaller than we thought but very beautiful. We walked into town and up to the palace where the guards dress similarly to the British royal guards but not as clipped as the Queen's ones, quite sloppy in fact. They don't march up and down, they sort of saunter. The Tivoli Gardens marching band put these guys to shame. I bet these Princess Mary would snap them into shape.

Coming back a very large ship was docked alongside us. It was the QE2. She was huge like a great blue whale and the same colour without the barnacles. Little Britanis looked like a tugboat next to her (but a lot prettier). I should have mentioned to their captain that a brighter coat of paint would do wonders for her.

Next day was Oslo and the town is close to the docks so we just a strolled in. This was the first day I didn't have to wear a coat.

Either I was getting used to the cooler days or it was warming up. Oslo is beautifully clean, and the shops are interesting. Val and I wandered through the park after having coffee and found the palace. This time the guards were marching outside. Maybe they heard my complaints about the neighbours and lifted their game. I do have influence you know.

I bought some pretty little ethnic socks and a beany for my friend who was having a baby. It was tempting to buy the drinking horn or even a Viking helmet, settled on a Troll instead. I heard that the locals actually believe in them. Each to their own, I guess, some people even believe in some sort of god. Superstitions are quite strange.

Theo the barman said he was passionately in love with me and told me to write and tell my mother. So, I did. George, the other barman said he loved me and then ate one of my chocolates, so I believe it's only cupboard love. I walked past the Staff Captain and the ship's agent and said "Hello Ladies" they looked at me with surprise and asked if they could prove they were men. I said to go right ahead but they only wanted to show me in the cabin, so I declined.

The next day we docked at Tilbury and time for me to leave. I planned to head for Dublin in a couple of days to visit people who were our neighbours in Australia. Then toss the dice and see what the world has to offer me this time.

## Chapter 27

# The Lady

## Saves the Day

*The Lady is one of Britain's weekly women's magazines.*
*It is particularly notable for its classified advertisements for Au Pairs.*

After dumping most of my stuff at Nan's apartment I rushed to the airport for my early morning Dublin flight, only to discover an unannounced plane strike. It was late evening before three plane loads of grumbling passengers (one of which was me) were herded into a jumbo jet and sent on our way.

I'd pre-warned Mike and Fran, the two people I was actually visiting, of the dilemma, and said I'd catch a cab to their house.

Luckily, once we landed I was asked to mind another passenger's bag whilst she relieved herself in the loo because over near the baggage carousel was Mike and sitting looking extremely rotund was heavily pregnant Fran.

A wonderful surprise but poor Fran burst into tears and said their house wasn't ready and had no room for me. Not to worry, they took me to a boarding house where I had the most enormous breakfast every day and then Mike or Fran or both of them would come and collect me and I made the rounds of all her family, where her mother would insist I needed more nourishment (I was beginning to think that Fran wasn't actually pregnant, just fat from all the food she was being force fed by her mum) then we'd go sightseeing and the evenings were filled with gaiety and noise like only a true Irish pub can produce.

An English magazine called 'The Lady' was filled with all sorts of girly stuff plus addresses for Au Pair jobs and agencies. I'd scour through this paper and also wrote to many agencies giving my Nan's address. Paris or somewhere in France was my preferred destination so with my fingers firmly crossed I hoped that by the time London was revisited a new career awaited.

Fran and Mike finally got the keys to their new home just as I was about to leave but taking one look at the amount of work that was needed, I knew it was time to roll up my sleeves and lend a hand.

Scrubbing, cleaning and cooking soon put paid to any guilt about freeloading and I loved being with these two fun-loving Irish folks. Fran even wrote to mum and asked if they could keep me.

Once the house was in a liveable state it was time to head back to

Blighty. Nan had a collection of letters from Au Pair agencies all with the same reply. No work going in France until September. Everyone was due to take their summer vacations and obviously the girls working there weren't going to cash in their employment just as a free trip to the French Riviera or somewhere else was on offer.

There was an offer for Greece though. OK, I can swear in Greek. That should come in handy. I had no one else craving my non-existent skills at child minding so Greece it had to be.

The Greek family I was to go to had four children from ages nine years down to eighteen months but the wife would also be there so she could steer me in the right direction. I figured that I had been a child once so how hard could looking after four of them be. If all else failed I could always serve them drinks I suppose.

First on my agenda was a trip up to London to cash in my pay slip from Chandris. It was quite a healthy load. Six months' pay in one lump sum, then over to the au pair agency to organize my bus fare and tickets. (I had to fork out for those myself) and gather up details of the meeting place in Greece, leaving on Friday and arriving Monday.

That was the plan anyway, but a slight hiccup put a spanner in the works.

Just as I was getting off the bus in Ealing heading back to Nan's a hand reached into my bag and relieved me of all my money plus bus and ferry tickets to Greece. The doors closed and away went my entire fortune in a blink of an eye.

Dumb Struck!! I couldn't believe it. I just stood there looking into the gaping hole in my handbag where just seconds ago held my future. What to do?

A London Bobby was just passing so I told him, he simply shrugged his shoulders and said it would be long gone by now.

Stranded!

I walked back to Nan's in a daze. What to do? She suggested firstly ringing the au pair agency and telling them what had just happened. Good advice as it turned out because they quickly cancelled all the travel tickets and organized another lot for the next departing day.

Nothing could be done about lost wages so the little I had left in the New South Wales bank was the only safety net I had.

Nan let me bunk up on her couch for the next few days and of course we headed for the local pubs each evening. They were always full of old people so when a young guy came over and started chatting it was a welcome change.

His name was Andy. We took off to another pub and this time the clientele was younger. I told Andy I'd lived in Ealing as a child, he asked if I remembered anyone from back then.

The only person I could think of was a guy called Alan Belson, a diabetic who was so brave being able to give himself injections. "The love of my life," at the time, when I was 5 or 6 years old. He had really been my brother's friend.

Beer spontaneously sprayed out of Andy's mouth with a burst of laughter. He knew Alan, and the best bit yet... He was coming to the pub this night. WOW!

True to his word, Alan turned up. Andy couldn't hold back the excitement of reintroducing me. But, oh what a pasty little fellow he was. There was no recognition and he looked somewhat perplexed about this strange girl standing in front of him, smiling and telling stories from long lost years.

Apparently, Alan had been in a nasty motor accident and lost his memory and was now recovering. He seemed to accept that what I said was true and we promised to write to each other, but we never did.

*Chapter 28*

# Greece

## What Was I Thinking?

*Greek Guard in Athens*

Saturday arrived. Nan and Pete took me to the bus station and waved me off.

This time the bus went to Belgium, Germany, Austria, Yugoslavia and then Greece. Instead of taking weeks it took days. The first night was a fitful sleep on the ferry, the second night in a cheap hotel in Austria.

The hotel only had one shower that we all lined up and took turns. One chap with a bit of initiative suggested showering with a friend to speed things up and offered to be my friend. I declined.

The third night was continuous driving and as we had two drivers it was safe enough. Apart from being boring the droning Greek music was making my ears bleed. I had some cassettes so handed them to the driver and to our relief he played them.

The bus was mainly full of young people with a smattering of oldies that were all good sports except one bloke who constantly complained and wanted to go faster. This didn't go down too well with our esteemed driver who actually stopped the bus completely and we thought there was going to be a punch up. That made life interesting anyway. Once heads cooled down we were back on our way, maybe slightly slower this time, or was I imagining it?

Arriving in Athens a lady from the au pair bureau met me and another girl called Helen. We found out that our two families were related and instead of staying in their winter homes in the city, we'd be taken to their summer bungalows complete with their own private beach in Ekklisia Agia Marina about an hour away.

The families were rich and well-travelled. Helen had one child and I had four to look after. We mainly worked together as the bungalows have a shared courtyard and they all got on with each other.

Warm weather meant the pebbly beach was in use daily. The two older boys, Angelo and Costa were easy. They spoke smatterings of English and wanted to learn more. They were happy with whatever games Helen and I could come up with and each afternoon everyone had a sleep.

I didn't actually have a bedroom just a camp bed in the lounge but as the children all went to bed early it wasn't a bother. The first week we all got to know each other with everyone on their best behaviour but it didn't take too long for the third boy in my family, Panagiotis, a four-year-old to become a real little shit.

Helen and I were given the same time off which were the afternoons on Tuesdays and full days on Fridays. On our first free afternoon we wandered into the nearest town, Varkiza. It was about seven kilometres away so quite a walk and we were hot and thirsty when we finally arrived.

The locals seemed to like the idea of two young ladies visiting and within no time we had six young men attending to our every need. Ice cream and cold drinks were supplied as well as personal tours whilst they jostled around trying to get our undivided attention.

We lapped it up and really appreciated the lift back home afterwards.

It was the two men in our au pair families who were related. They were brothers. Helen's boss was a black belt karate instructor who supplied lessons out the back in a courtyard of the bungalows a couple of times a week. He's a bit of a show-off to tell the truth. Quite different to the father of my four children. Both the women are gentle and easy going although I think Helen's woman is used as a doormat to her ever preening husband, but she adores him so who knows?

The families quite often had friends visiting in the evening and although Helen and I are invited we were also charged with the job of cleaning up afterwards. This got a bit wearisome when the guests didn't go home until about three in the morning and we had to keep up with the children early. I also couldn't go to bed until they all left because where my bed was situated.

By the second week the niceties began to tarnish, and the children grew horns. They'd swear a lot in Greek. I hadn't taught them any of those words. HONESTLY! But I used to tell the third one to "Go drown yourself" a few times.

Thank god it's Friday. As the saying goes. Helen and I met another au pair called Karen who works up the road. Her family were lovely and when they found out about Helen and I they made sure Karen had the same days off as us. We'd all head into Athens which was about forty kilometres away by bus.

The first Friday Helen was to meet her boss so Karen and I wandered around the markets stopping for cool drinks at café's. We met a couple of guys both called Peter and they took us to dinner that night.

During the day I kept running into people I knew. It was weird. Two from our resent bus trip but also three from the Australis. We were having such a great time that we missed the last bus back so whiled away the hours at a disco until five in the morning when the bus service started up again. Snatched a quick two hours sleep before the rigors of the day started over.

The following week I only had the Thursday afternoon off instead of the Friday as both parents were going out. I rang one of the Peter's up and he met me in Athens. We did the whole tourist trip around the Acropolis then after a cooling drink took the train to Piraeus. It was a mad dash to get back to Athens in time to jump on the last bus home at midnight. I made it that time.

The following Tuesday the three of us girls headed into Athens again. We were getting pretty good at this. Helen disappeared to meet up with a friend. Karen and I started off at the flea markets and then it was time to watch the changing of the guards. I actually saw it this time and it was as funny as I'd been told. They sort of half skip and half dance at the same time do a silly walk. One of the guards tripped and everyone laughed, poor sod.

Our wanderings took us to the top of Mount Lycabettus. Had we done our homework or simply been more observant we would have noticed the funicular railway, instead we traipsed up the ever-rising road. The afternoons get really hot and our faces were dripping with sweat by the time we reached the summit.

Mountaineering on a thirty plus degree day isn't recommended, especially as it hadn't been planned. The inner sanctum of St George Chapel was inviting, only they wouldn't let us in. That hussy of a girl, Karen, was showing a bit of bare shoulder. The dilemma was thwarted by draping my newly purchased dress over the offending body parts.

It was a cool respite in this ancient building, so after a good look around and our body temperatures had returned to normal we took our prepacked picnic lunch of pumpernickel bread and chunks of cheese to be eaten and shared with the local pussy cats under the shade of a tree in the nearby park.

Work as an au pair wasn't what I thought it would be. I seemed to be employed more as a house cleaner than a child minder. The dishes were always left for me to deal with and then when an aunt came to mind the children when the family went out for the day, I had to do all the cleaning. Add to this I was told by Karen's employer that I should have been paid double what they were giving me. No wonder they were rich. At least the days off were fun.

Instead of always relying on a very unreliable bus service to take us into Athens, Karen and I decided to hitch hike instead. Helen had gone away to a Greek Island with her family, lucky thing. A fellow picked us up and chatting along the way I found out he was ex crew from the Australis and had left three years before me. He was so excited to meet an old crew member that he took us out for lunch then to another place for coffee, so we didn't get into Athens until about six at night. I wish I could remember his name. He gave me his phone number but that has been lost many moons ago.

We were sitting at an outdoor café with our ice cream sodas when two guys pulled up in their snazzy sports car. They oozed charisma and charm and asked us to meet them outside the King George hotel at ten. We never went, we could tell sleaze bags from a hundred paces by then.... or so we thought. Instead we headed back to Varkiza, stopped for a drink, met an Italian guy who offered us a lift home which we accepted and were actually home at the earliest time yet. Just gone midnight.

The children I looked after had absolutely no fear of water. Even the baby took off at a hundred miles an hour and I had to charge after her to make sure her shoes at least came off.

One day we were playing in the water when a Willy Willy, sort of micro whirl wind whipped up and grabbed all of our stuff and dumped it in the water. Unfortunately, the watch Bill had given me for my twenty first birthday wasn't as safely tucked into a shoe as I thought and that also went for a dunking. It stopped working straight away and didn't start again until a few years later when I finally took it to be repaired.

Panagiotis learnt to climb up on the kitchen bench to reach the sweets his mum had hidden from the children. He was up there like a mountain goat and impossible to control. If I'd had a rope, I would have tied him up (or strung him up). He always managed to do disastrous things when I was changing the baby or busy doing something else or even worse just when his parents arrived.

He also liked to sneak into the bathroom when I was showering or getting changed. Another little trick was trying to pull my bikini off when we were playing in the sea. Little perve. I wrote to mum and said he was either going to grow up to be a mass murderer or rapist, or both.

Our days off took us further afield. Karen and I explored a lot of Athens and took trains to Piraeus and then we found out about a wine festival that was ongoing until September.

We took a bus to Daphne which was about ten kilometres from Athens. Paid fifty drachmas which was the entry fee and handed a plastic cup. This enabled us to taste test or glug as much wine as we wanted.

Greek music was playing, people dragged you up to dance, food stalls offered sustenance and the hot night air was electric. I decided to tell every guy that I met a different story as to why I was in Greece. It was so funny, sometimes I'd be a lawyer, a banker, fashion designer and my favourite was a deep-sea diver/marine biologist studying the sinking city of Venice. I was believed as well until two groups of guys met up and I'd told them completely different stories. They got a bit peeved.

Coming back on the bus to Athens was past midnight which meant we'd already missed our connecting bus home. Then, **BANG!** A flat tyre so everyone piled out and we all shared taxis. Three fellows took Karen and I to a disco but we didn't like them much so we left.

Unfortunately, they followed us, and we got a bit scared. We turned on them and in our most unladylike way told them to "PISS OFF!!!" which they did. Luckily, we found an all-night café so were ordered pizza and coffee and sat there until time for the bus to wake up and take us home.

The families hired boats and they said they would teach Helen and I water skiing but as it turned out we just looked after the children whilst they played with their new toys. Meanwhile my charges were in another room sounding like they were murdering each other. I gave it a while hoping they'd do a good job before I investigated. ...No Blood. No one dead, oh well. Never mind.

Sometimes we three girls had different days off because of the commitments of the families. Whenever I had time to myself, I'd quite often just walk into Varkiza. It was a lovely seaside town and I'd got to know a few locals and felt safe there.

One day I was walking home when a car pulled up and offered me a lift. I said I was just about at my destination and the guy said he'd seen me in town and would have offered me a lift earlier if he knew I had to walk all this way. Never mind. He was cute too. He asked me to telephone him on my next day off which I would have done if the telephones hadn't all died. A missed opportunity.... maybe?

Helen hadn't been out very often with Karen and I. She had an American friend that she'd meet so we'd go our separate ways. However, one day she did come to Athens and stayed with me. We went to Plaka and I showed her places that Karen and I had discovered. She hadn't seen all that much of Athens which I was quite surprised about. Usually American tourists or even ones that live here really get around.

We then caught a bus into Daphne and we both played my stupid game of pretending we were someone else. She even changed her name to Veronica or Ronny for short. We were from Canada, America, Australia, England but when she said she was from Japan I had to bite the inside of my cheek to stop from laughing, that wasn't quite as believable.

We were students, florists, politicians anything but never au pairs. We'd be chatted up by guys and tell them we'd meet them some place and never turn up, dance with everyone and then just bugger off. We did accept a lift from one guy close to closing time and he took us to an amusement park.

We rode the ghost train and bumper cars and as the place was closing, he took us to a disco in a town called Glyfada which was on the way home, well towards that direction anyway and then actually took us home by three in the morning.

Next day when we were getting ready for the beach. I noticed a bruise on Helen's back. She tried to hide it which roused my suspicions, so I asked her out right how she got it. With that, she broke down and cried and said her horrible employer had done that to her. The bruise was much larger than I first thought, and it was like a purple handprint. He had been molesting her and now given her the ultimatum of either sleeping with him or leaving.

The BASTARD!!

Helen was only nineteen years old and her first time away from home. She thought an au pair job would be a safe adventure not a constant sexual battleground. To make things worse, the wife of this creature was lovely and idolised her prick of a husband. The guy had an ego big enough to scale a mountain. We had to do something.

*Chapter 29*

# Moonlight Flit

## The Escape

*Donkeys and old priest in Greece*

Tuesday Helen and I went into Athens together. We had long secret talks about how to solve this problem and the only thing we came up with was to run away.

Helen didn't want to hurt the feelings of Iphigenia, the wife of the bastard, so an escape plan has to be devised.

First, we worked out our finances which didn't actually amount to much but if we pooled them, we could get as far as a bus to Paris. Not much more thought went into that. We booked it. Leave on Thursday which was only two days away.

Sitting in a café we were approached by two American soldiers. There was an army base near Athens and these guys had been here for a while. During the conversation, (which was all in English and actually understood for a change) we told them of our plans.

Only problem, which happened to be immense, was how to get to Athens without the families noticing that we were never coming back. The answer. These guys offered to collect us at two in the morning. They would then take us to their apartment where we could rest up and then make our way to the bus station by two in the afternoon and we'd be on our way.

How perfect was that? The guys also said they could be trusted because if they did anything to us and we reported them they would have too much to lose. We spent the whole day with these guys. Bowling, eating and to a disco before they drove us all the way home, so they knew where to collect us in two night's time. They even offered to give us some money, but we refused that.

We couldn't tell Karen of our plans because if she honestly didn't know she would never be compromised. It was a tough decision because we had become quite close to her and our friendship was real.

Helen demanded that her boss pay her the money he owed her and luckily, he did which turned out to be the same amount as her bus fare. My boss had been paying me regularly, so we now had about the same amount of cash. We'd change the money in Athens to travellers' cheques on Thursday.

'D Day'. Well 'D Night' anyway.

We'd secretly packed and had everything ready but the families just wouldn't bugger off like they usually did. Even the afternoon siesta wasn't happening. Then early evening we got a break and as quickly and quietly as we could our suitcases were taken up near the rubbish bins, just inside the gate wall and hidden behind crates. The night passed as normal, but I know my heart and possibly Helen's was beating so hard it could have joined an orchestra.

Why wouldn't they go to bed? I yawned and showed tiredness so they would go away, but they just ignored it. Everyone knew I couldn't go to sleep until they retired because of where my bed was.

Helen and I met outside for emergency talks. We couldn't walk up the driveway and out the gate because we'd be seen, worse came to worse, we'd have to scale the wall at the back which lead onto the road. This is what we eventually did. Then waited....and waited.....Lena's car (she was the mother of my four little darlings) started and we realized that they had twigged on to our escape plan.

Dived into the bushes and just lay low. Her car was gone for ages and then finally returned. We still kept hidden. Eventually they went to bed.

Now what to do? The bus wouldn't come for hours yet and we'd definitely be caught in daylight. Then just around the bend a taxi appeared. It was like a miracle. We hailed it down, scrambled to retrieve our hidden suitcases and off we went. The taxi driver was only going as far as Varkiza but that was on the way so it would do. Plus, we didn't want to spend all our money on a taxi to Athens. We could take the bus in the morning. Meanwhile we found beach chairs and tried to make ourselves as comfortable as possible and sleep with one eye open.

Sleeping on a Greek beach had been done before but last time I had a sleeping bag. This time only a hard suitcase and a million midges eating us. I was itchy and scratchy, but Helen was their main meal. She was covered in lumps and bumps and itched like crazy. I think when we boarded the bus next morning, they must have thought we had the plague.

It was still too early for banks or money change places when we arrived in Athens but the public toilets were open so we could go in there and freshen up a bit which cooled my skin but didn't do much to alleviate Helen's suffering.

When the travel agency opened, we left our luggage and wandered around saying goodbye to Athens and buying enough supplies for three days. August in Athens is as hot as opening an oven door and we knew the three-day bus ride wasn't going to be pleasant if it was anything like the one coming over. Worse in fact because the temperature would have been easily twenty degrees cooler back then.

Panic set in again when the bus wasn't there. We thought we'd missed it but it was hours late instead. Our seats were directly on top of the heaters which they hadn't turned off. Heat spots erupted adding to the discomfort of midge bites.

It was impossible to sleep on the seats unless you were a contortionist, so we gave that up and kept ourselves amused by playing silly games. At four in the morning the bus stopped in Bologna and they turfed everyone out. We weren't to come back until nine. This was an unexpected surprise for everyone. They did stop at an unfinished or maybe falling down hotel, but we didn't have money put aside for that.

Luckily some girls on the bus knew of our plight and sneakily snuck us into their room. They had two singles and a double so plenty of room for us all. Also allowed us to freshen up with a much needed shower.

.

# Chapter 30
# M.I.J.E.
## Paris

*Helen and I in Paris outside the youth hostel where we stayed all those years ago. We met up again after 37 years and our friendship continued as if we'd never been apart.*

The bus was now hours behind schedule and instead of arriving in Paris on Sunday we finally fell off exhausted, dazed and lost on Monday.

Here we were in Paris. *The City of Love.* It proved to be true, as one thing is for sure, Helen can be sweaty, spotty and sticky but still absolutely gorgeous. Her big blue eyes, fiery red locks and tall slender body caused tongues to loll out and help was offered for this damsel in distress before we'd even alighted from the bottom step of the bus. I followed like a puppy.

First it was one fellow who tried to help us find accommodation. He straight away offered a chivalrous hand and carried her suitcase. I struggled along behind. It took three attempts and a couple more willing helpers, one of which gallantly took my suitcase before a youth hostel was open and had vacancies.

August in Paris is holiday time for the locals but thanks to these guys we finally had a place to rest our weary heads. Well not until three in the afternoon anyway, so we plonked our cases down and headed out in search of a coffee.

To our delight we were just around the corner from Notre Dame Cathedral and cafes. The gang of guys who had grown in number were beginning to become pains in the bum jostling for our attention and we poor tired things just wanted quiet. We thanked them profusely and basically told them in the politest possible way all to bugger off as we eventually made our way back to the hostel and by the time we got there and produced all appropriate paperwork and money we were allowed in.

Showered and a change of clothes recharged our batteries. The choices of bunk beds in a dormitory sorted. Suitcases secured in lockers so off we went.

The Champs-Elysees wasn't too far away so up one side and down the other we asked for work in every bar and shop. Helen could speak a smattering of French and I had none whatsoever. The chances of finding a job with those credentials was zero.

Back to the hostel and we slept like the dead.

Next morning after a large bowl of steaming hot chocolate, a third of a baguette with jam which was breakfast and included in the price of a bed, we took to the streets again. We were told of employment agencies so headed for those. We walked and marvelled at this beautiful city but came back without even a whisper of any job opportunities. I'd offered a little prayer in Sacre Coeur all to no avail. That did it. I knew I was an atheist for some good reason.

Next day we travelled by the Metro to a French shipping line and also the American Express offices but still no luck.

The Paris Metro is a subterranean world of its own. A maze of tunnels and escalators. A world hidden from the beauty of the city above.

Chatelet metro station is immense, you can sometimes hear African drumming thumping its vibrant sounds through the cave like networks of corridors, an accordionist playing 'Flight of the bumblebee 'with passion and perfection or a lone singer testing out the acoustics. You can hear them but can't find them; turn a corner and there they are. The city was casting a spell on us.

The evenings in the hostel are brilliant. I didn't realize how much fun everyone had. I should have though when you think about it. Everyone is a traveller with many stories to tell and cares left behind the last place they stayed. So many nationalities, yet we all want hot chocolate or coffee with a baguette for breakfast. There were musicians busking their way around Europe, art students copying the masters in the Louvre, rich kids with daddy's money to burn and people like us.

In the evenings impromptu parties erupt. People share their experiences both good and bad with warnings best heeded. Laughter comes easily before the dormitories fall into silence when exhausted young people succumb to sleep.

We'd been here a few days and the money was getting tight. If we didn't get work soon, we wouldn't even be able to afford the youth hostel and we had only been eating breakfast, nothing else so cutting down on food and drink wasn't even an option.

I asked daily of anyone who cared to listen if they knew of any work going. John-Paul the manager of M.I.J.E. finally took pity on us and we both got jobs at the youth hostel. I worked as a chambermaid and Helen on reception. Her French was coming back luckily but I had no idea of the language. We still only make enough to stay the night and have breakfast but after a couple of weeks people begin to notice how we are looking gaunt. I was cutting my baguette up into small bite sized chunks and lathering on butter and jam then rationing myself small pieces all throughout the day. Not sure what Helen was doing but finally Alain, a guy who also worked at the hostel asked us out for dinner and when we nearly ate the tablecloth as well, he realized quite how starving we were.

Word got around and dinner invitations started pouring in. Sometimes we were invited together sometimes separately. No matter what though, we were being looked after. Alain took me home to meet his parents and we had a fondue. It was a great talking point and they all spoke English.

Jean-Paul was my boss and he took me away for the weekend to a moto cross rally. We left with another guy called Ali on Saturday morning and headed way into the country arriving at five in the afternoon. John-Paul's brother works for Moto Review and the whole weekend was paid for by that magazine.

I was supposed to be selling books, hats and other advertising memorabilia but as I couldn't speak the language, I was sent off buying drinks and sandwiches. We had great fun. Seven o'clock in the morning the track was hosed down by the fire trucks to make it muddy and sloshy but by the time the sun was up, the track became a dust bowl and we were covered in red brick coloured dust. I was given a complementary ticket so could wander anywhere to get the best vantage places. So exciting.

The day ended at seven at night then the packing up began. Everything was filthy and dusty, us included. Wearily we climbed into the van. Ali turned the key but nothing. The van had gone on strike. It took another hour of fiddling with it before we hit the road. We stopped for dinner along the way when we saw a restaurant full of bikers and joined in the fun. A water fight happened, and nobody was spared. The dust once again became mud but this time it was inside a building. I bet the owners were thrilled.

The drive back to Paris was a long one and I fell asleep in the van only to be woken by an enormous blast and choking fumes. The exhaust pipe had broken, black smoke engulfed us. Nowhere to get it fixed at that hour on a Sunday evening meant a slow crawl back with all the windows open.

Helen and I were earning four hundred and twenty Francs a week and our room and breakfast was three hundred and fifty Francs a week. We desperately needed to find somewhere cheaper. We considered staying in a cheap hotel, but we'd have to share a bed, and everyone would think we were queer, and we wouldn't be getting breakfast so that was a *No Go* idea. I also wanted to start going to school to learn French because the language just wasn't sifting into my brain naturally.

A saving grace came in the form of two people. One was Vicky, an Australian/French girl. Her French father had died a few years ago but she was mainly brought up in Australia with her mum. She spoke the language fluently and was travelling around Europe having a break from university. An instant friendship sprung up between the three of us. The other was a fellow called Marc who worked at M.I.J.E. but was leaving the area and had a cheap flat ready to be vacated.

So here we were, three girls all in our early twenties. Helen the ravishing Red Head with looks to die for, Vicky the fun loving, French speaking, blonde with the brains and me, the mad friend everyone has to have. Let loose on the unsuspecting Parisians.

Helen, Vicky and I decided to take over the rent of Marc's flat. It was on the eighth floor and was only one room with a sink a window and a chest of drawers. Nothing else, well a packet of condoms but I think he was just showing off.

Back in the old days this would have been the servant's quarters so that seemed fitting, especially for me. We had no beds but with the aid of Alain and his brother's car, a blind eye from Jean-Paul we borrowed two single mattresses, sheets, blankets and pillows from the hostel and carted them across town and up the elevator to our humble abode.

During the day the mattresses were placed one on top of the other, this was our couch. At night they were reconfigured into a double bed and the three of us shared, not worried about being called Queer now. This was desperation living at its best, or maybe worst.

It turned out that I was the most horrible person to sleep with because I rolled so much and constantly shoved the others off the bed. Luckily, we were on the floor and not in a bunk. They were not happy with me. We still used the showers at the hostel, and I would swap the sheets for newly laundered ones each week. Our other clothes we took to the launderette.

Buying a monthly Carte De Orange metro ticket saved us a bit of money and the metro was a good place to catch up on my letter writing or book reading.

It seemed like a good place for creepy men to get cheap thrills as well. A leg rub on a crowded train might not always be as innocent as first thought. Or someone looking over your shoulder and seeing English writing and then they announce that they LUUVVVE you.

I had a trick or two up my sleeve for these situations. I would either yell in a very loud voice "Do you mind!" or turn my head away, colour a few teeth in with black eyebrow pencil and then give the offender a toothless grin. Both worked. They would alight at the very next stop.

Vicky had found herself a job in a travel agency. She managed to score trips to Venice, Rome or other beautiful cities. Helen did a disappearing act and took off to Nice for a while and I now went to Alliance Francaise, a school to learn French in the evenings but still kept on cleaning and making beds during the day.

Coming home late at night quite often meant I'd get followed. It could have been a coincidence as many people walk in the same direction but sometimes not. One time I heard the familiar footfall of a follower. I turned and saw a man come into my building. I called the elevator and when it arrived, I opened the old-fashioned iron grill door and stepped in.

Politely I held the door open for the man only to discover he was having a fun time playing with his old fella and drooling (from his mouth). Quickly I slammed the gate closed and pressed the button for the fifth floor and run up the next three flights of stairs just in case he tried to follow me.

As the winter crept upon us our little room was freezing. If we had any hand washing and hung it out the window in the evening, it would be rock hard and frozen the next morning.

Not all things were creepy and bad though. We'd also found a phone box that you could rewire and make free phone calls home. An Italian guy discovered it and showed me how to wrap some electrical wire around the cord, put in forty centimes, dial and then when the receiver picks up quickly shove the other end of electrical wire into the mouthpiece. You had to talk loudly to hear over the constant buzzing, but it was great to hear voices from home. When the call had finished and the handset back in its cradle the forty centimes returned. Problem was, whenever one of these phones was discovered a crowd of travellers would soon find out about it and a queue would form which made the authorities suspicious. Fun while it lasted though.

Between the three of us we had gathered quite a few new friends. John-Francoise was a twenty-eight-year-old pharmacist and he had a bit of a fan base with many females. He was fit and good looking plus a rugby player and possibly rich. His semi live in lover was a tour guide and she would be away for weeks at a time, plenty of time for the debonair JF to meet new belles.

I was one of his conquests and he introduced me to marijuana. The first time I smoked it I didn't think it had any effect until we went for a drive in his beautiful Citroen car and I felt all the traffic was coming straight for us and we'd have a head on collision. Of course, we were on the wrong side of the road as far as I was concerned but my brain went into panic overdrive and I vomited.

After that we only smoked at his place, but it was a feeling I never enjoyed. He had his advantages though, all we girls got the birth control pills for nothing the whole time we lived in Paris, there was always a stash in the boot of his car.

Another friend I made was Alison. She was a Blue Bell dancer at the Lido, and we met during a French class as she's Australian. She said there may be a chance that I could work as a dresser. So after school one night we went together.

The girls change rooms are a mad confusion of bright skimpy costumes and enormous feathered head gear that weigh a ton, dusty clouds of stage makeup and half naked women shuffling around in haste getting ready for the night's performances.

Alison took me to the woman in charge but unfortunately there was no work available, but I could stay and watch the show. Being tall and slim Alison tried to talk me into having lessons and joining the show girls. It was a quite a compliment, but I never had the nerve. Another opportunity missed.

*Chapter 31*

# Are You Local?

## A Place to Call Home

*Helen, Bernard and I (as we were then) We are all still friends*

Vicky had found an apartment that needed us. The family who owned it were going to America for eight months and wanted house sitters. The place was a fully furnished two-bedroom apartment with a pull-out divan in the lounge which would be the third bed. It came with bedding and towels, in fact everything, we just needed Helen to return.

Where the hell was, she? I was beginning to worry. Her parents had taken off overseas for nine months around the world trip on her father's ship and I felt sort of responsible for her. The police were no help at all. They said as she was over eighteen, she could do as she pleased. I was concerned that she might turn up in a ditch somewhere with her throat cut.

One day the periodical friend returned. I gave her a hug and then belted her for worrying me. She now had to look for another job and we all had to pay three months' rent in advance for this perfect apartment. Vicky could afford it and could put a share in for Helen, I asked for a loan from Mum and Dad. Between us we raised the cash and by December we had returned the borrowed mattresses and sheets and moved into a more comfortable abode.

Paris is divided into arrondissement or numbered boroughs. There is local snobbery surrounding the area you live in just like everywhere so leaving the fourth arrondissement and moving to the seventeenth could have been seen as a step in the wrong direction but not as far as we were concerned. We actually had a bed each! YIPPEE!!

This area had quite a few Arabs which the Parisians tended to look down on. We were warned it could be sleazy and dangerous but in fact we found it quite the opposite. Once the locals realized who these three beauties were, they looked out for us especially when we got home late at night. The local patisseries had the usual delicious croissants made fresh every morning, so breakfast was sorted, and we were happy.

My cleaning job brought about some fun times. Meeting all sorts of people and going out together after work. Sometimes making Apple Pie Beds' for cheeky hostel guests and paying for it the next day when they caught me. (Apple Pie bed was a bed which, as a practical joke, has been made with one of the sheets folded back on itself so that a person's legs cannot be stretched out.) I did this to a German teacher who came to Paris with his school group on an excursion. Next day he snuck back into the hostel and when I was cleaning the shower, he pushed me in, and I got drenched.

Sometimes I'd get sweets and chocolates occasionally a tip (from Americans) but one time a fellow from Thailand who made his own jewellery left me a beautiful silver and blue sapphire ring because I'd admired his work. He actually wanted me to buy something from him, but my funds didn't stretch that far so the next day this gift was left in an envelope on his pillow for me.

The Latin Quarter was a favourite meeting place. It was lively and food was tasty. Students would cram into cheap and cheerful restaurants where waiters could hold up to fifteen full meal plates at once. You dare not get in their way and somehow, they managed to navigate the maze of crowded tables and remember where each meal belonged. Watching them was an entertainment.

For some reason Vicky would always be the victim of a bum pinch. She was getting so annoyed with it one night that she said if anyone else did it to her she was going to punch him, and she did. She landed a full-bodied blow right on the overly large Arab nose that the pinching fingers belonged to. Everyone cheered.

I met a gorgeous guy called Bernard. He was fun with a touch of madness and I fell for him hook, line and sinker. Only problem was he had to do his national service and my days off didn't always coincide with his. He also couldn't speak English and my French wasn't all that brilliant, but we made up our own language and mimed a lot as well.

When we did get days off together, he would borrow a car and head to places like Normandy or small country market towns. Sometimes it was train trips to the zoo or picnics in forests but most of the time it was Paris discos or nightclubs. He would turn up unannounced with baskets of vegetables and we'd have a cook up and watch TV.

Vicky had met a lovely Frenchman also. Her mother had warned her about them and said never to get involved but it was too late. She was smitten. Helen also had a beau so the six of us would sometimes all hang out together if our days off happened together, or if I took a sickie.

One evening a group of us were wandering along the Champs-Elysées and we called into what looked like a car show room, which it was but also an eatery called Pub Renault. I was wearing Bernard's army jumper because I liked it and it was huge on me. We ordered ice-cream sundaes which were served up in tall glasses sitting on plates which advertised the name of the pub. I really wanted the plate so when no one was looking I shoved it up my jumper and simply walked out with it. The beauty of being flat-chested. I still have that souvenir today.

We three girls were all about the same size and constantly swapped clothes. It got to the stage where we couldn't remember who bought what. It was a nuisance when you'd planned on wearing something only to find it adorning another body or even worse, scrunched up and dirty.

The afro permanent wave was in fashion and I thought it would suit me. As it turned out, it didn't. I looked like a mix between a mop and a poodle. Ghastly! So, one night when the girls were asleep, I attacked my hair with a pair of scissors and chopped down to about one-inch lengths, coloured it with henna and was quite pleased with my new Pixie look. Next morning, I was dressed in jeans and Bernard's army jumper when Helen sleepily walked past the kitchen and screamed. She thought I was some bloke who'd broken in. Not quite the reaction I was after.

As my French was improving due to all the lessons I was having, Vicky decided that it was time to get a better job. I agreed but had no idea what else I could do.

We searched through the papers each day until and there it was; English speaking person needed for the Sheraton Hotel. I applied and Helen came with me for moral support when it was interview time.

All dressed up and looking elegant in I went, asked to speak to the manager, simply said "Bonjour" and she took one look at me and said "No'. I was devastated. When we got back to our apartment and told

Vicky she was on the phone in an instant. God knows what she said to them, but I started work the following Monday.

The wages more than doubled what I'd been earning as a cleaner and this time I was a waitress. The menus were written in French with English translations underneath so some people would simply point, some would ask in English and some brave souls would ask in French. I simply learnt to follow their eyes until my French menu reading was perfected.

I loved playing tricks on English speaking people who naturally thought I was French, and they would order in even more woeful French than I had. I wouldn't let on that I could speak English and they were always thrilled that they got whatever they believed they'd ordered (I'd hear what they really wanted even if they ordered incorrectly in French). The whole meal would continue, and I'd only speak French to them until just as they were about to go I'd say "Thanks very much" in my lovely Aussie accent.

Often, we'd get tour groups and the food would be specially selected *Authentic French Cuisine.* Snails in garlic butter! Ahh, YUK! The stink was horrendous, and ninety percent of the dishes would go untouched.

The chefs and waiting staff would all dread it. Plus they were difficult to carry out to the table even though they were served in specially made little metal dishes with indented semi circles for the snail shells to supposedly sit in snugly, but the horrible things would roll around like marbles and quite often roll right off the plate onto the floor.

A large group of Australians' came in one day. Luckily for them they didn't get the Caterer's Special, they could all order from the menu.

I could hear the accents and found out they were on **The Women's Weekly World Discovery Tour.** I quickly taught a little French waitress to go out and say "Good áy mate, ow yr go-win?' to the whole group. They burst out laughing and wanted to know who the Aussie was.

I went out and said hello. They were the most delightful ladies and I found out they were from Black Rock in Victoria which wasn't far from

Mum and Dad's home. They all promised to ring my parents when their holiday was over, and they actually did.

I mastered the art of looking French even though I still couldn't speak it without an English accent and got the grammar wrong most of the time.

Waitressing in five-inch heels was a given and they made my legs look extremely long. A customer said I had beautiful legs, I just said "I know 'and walked off. The look on his face was priceless. Later he asked me to go to bed with him, I said no because I wasn't tired, so he said seductively that there were other things we could do. I said yes throw darts at the ceiling. He laughed and left me a ten franc tip, so no harm done.

On the first of September our eight months of house sitting duties was up and we had to find somewhere else to live. Vicki had already moved out and was sharing a flat with her boyfriend and his mates. Their flat was going to become vacant about the same time so Helen and I jumped the queue and we moved in. All very convenient. This time we were on the fifth floor in a completely different area of Paris. Thank goodness the metro maps are easy to read, or I would have been hopelessly lost.

We only had one set of keys and at night the concierge would lock the large external doors and our apartment buzzer didn't work. Well, it was bound to happen. Either Helen or I would one day be locked out. Luckily for me it was her. I patiently waited at the window but as it got later and later and still no sign of my wayward friend, I fell asleep. Next morning a rude awakening by thumping on the door I shakily opened up to find a furious red head with steam coming out of her ears. She'd had to spend the night in a sleazy hotel and was not pleased. That'll teach her to come home late.

Working at the Sheraton meant I also had to take my turn at the late shift and Montparnasse metro station can be a lonely place waiting for the last train. I began to recognise the warning signs.

If a man standing near the platform entrance wearing a raincoat quickly turns away from me and then just as I have to pass he turns around furiously masturbating I would not show fear or shock, instead I would stand right in front of him and clap my hands in wondrous applause, sometimes even shouting Bravo! The offending winky would shrivel and become insignificant and the metro entertainer would slink away.

It was nearing four years that I'd been away from home, all except for the two months back a couple of years ago. Vicki was returning to her Melbourne home to continue her university studies whilst her guy had to do his military service.

They planned to meet back in Australia when he'd completed it. Helen and Bernard both wanted to come over, but they were having difficulties getting visas for longer than three months. I had a visa in a British passport so maybe the answer was to get an Aussie passport and somehow, I could sponsor my two friends. I also needed to do something about furthering my very lacking education.

Not quite sure what I wanted to do

Maybe hairdressing.

Time would tell.

# About the author

Jennifer eventually returned to Melbourne where she met and married David, had two sons, and many animals made their way into the family home.

She did become a hairdresser and even taught it for a few years. Finding hidden talents in her hands she found that set design, costume making, woodwork and even electronics led her into a career as a technician. Stranger things have happened!

Jennifer and her mum rediscovered the delights of sea travel in 2013 on a cruise around new Zealand. This time there were no secrets.

Jennifer's Aussie flatmate, Vicky, married her Frenchman and lives most of her time in Melbourne.

Facebook reunited lost friendships, and 37 years after their adventures, Helen and Jennifer met at Gatwick airport and flew off to Turkey together where they once again became the mad 20 year olds that lurked just beneath the surface. It didn't end there, either. They both went back to Paris and stayed the weekend with Jennifer's old boyfriend, Bernard, and his gorgeous partner, Nellie.

Printed in Australia
AUHW012012260919
317860AU00001B/2